Country Crafts and Craftsmen

Garry Hogg
COUNTRY CRAFTS AND CRAFTSMEN

Illustrated by

KATHLEEN DANCE

Hutchinson of London

HUTCHINSON & CO. (*Publishers*) LTD
178-202 Great Portland Street, London, W.1

London Melbourne Sydney
Auckland Bombay Toronto
Johannesburg New York

First published 1959

This book has been set in Bembo type face. It has been printed in Great Britain by The Anchor Press, Ltd., in Tiptree, Essex, on Smooth Wove paper and bound by Taylor Garnett Evans & Co., Ltd., in Watford, Herts

# Contents

Introduction

ONE of the important ways in which Man differs from even the most highly developed and intelligent of animals lies in his capacity to utilize materials that are ready to hand, and to invent tools that will enable him to turn them to his greater advantage. He may be less fleet of foot than the deer, less agile than the monkey, have less power of endurance than the wolf or the camel and be less adaptable to changes of climate than innumerable creatures that have learned to survive extremes of temperature; but he vastly surpasses all animals in other and not less vital kinds of adaptability.

From the very dawn of his history, during all the thousands of years in which he has lived on the earth, he has been steadily developing the art of utilizing materials in ever-extending fields of activity. Wanting something better than tree or cave for a residence, he learned to pile stones together in such a way as to protect him and keep him snug and warm. Where there were no stones ready to his hand, he discovered that clay could be hardened in the sun in the form of rough bricks every bit as good as stone.

He found that the antlers of deer made excellent picks, the shoulder-blades of oxen excellent spades. He found that flint made excellent tools for shaping other natural materials. With every new discovery, or invention—for in prehistoric times they were much the same thing—some new field of activity was opened up for him.

As Man's needs became more numerous and complex, he began to find that the materials which had sufficed his ancestors for all their needs were no longer adequate for the ever-growing

7

variety of his demands. He brought more and more ingenuity to the invention or adaptation of implements and tools, but found that it was not only new tools he required: he had need of new materials. In many centuries of discovery he had exhausted the variety of raw materials at his disposal—the timber, the stone, the mineral ores and the rest; now he must set to work and invent and produce a whole new range of raw materials.

It is in the present century that this new phase of his activity has been widely demonstrated for the first time, though there were hints of it in the previous century. This mid-twentieth century, which you may call the Atomic Age, or the Sputnik Age, or the Zeta Age, or by any other name which denotes outstanding work in invention by scientists in many fields of scientific research, is the age in which Man has shown most startlingly his ability to go one better than Nature. In fact, it might be called simply the Synthetic Age.

If Macbeth were living today he might well repeat what Shakespeare made him say after he had met the Weird Sisters on the blasted heath: 'Nothing is but what is not'. For today it is difficult, often quite impossible, for the person who is not an expert to know whether what he is looking at really is what it appears to be, or whether in fact it is something completely different.

That snug-looking 'fur' coat, for example, may well not be the skin of an animal at all but some form of synthetic. It is very likely made of nylon; and nylon itself is made of synthetic chemicals derived either from petroleum or from coal or from agricultural waste. These same waste products made those sheer, filmy, transparent stockings, and those immensely strong tow-ropes used when aircraft tow gliders, and those thin, tough, light-weight ropes used by men climbing in the Himalayas; and a hundred and more other common objects of everyday life!

Until quite recently, scent manufacturers depended entirely on natural sources of supply. To make one ounce of 'violet oil', the basis of one of their scents, it was necessary to crush twenty-five tons of violet petals! Attar of roses, used for certain scents, was becoming increasingly scarce and proportionately dear as the demand increased, and the point was reached when the manufacturers had to turn to the chemist and ask him to evolve a synthetic 'violet oil' or other base. Today it is done quickly, cheaply and easily; and only the specialist expert can detect the difference between the real and the synthetic. 'Fruit' juices and confectionery flavours, with alluring names and pictures of the fruit they represent, are more often than not the products of the chemist's retorts, test-tubes and bunsen-burners!

Iron has been known to Man for thousands of years, steel for generations; but today, with the incessant demand for greater and greater speeds, it has become necessary to evolve alloys possessing special properties. Certain alloys can withstand immensely high temperatures; others combine great strength with extreme lightness; others are so hard and tough that special tools have had to be devised for cutting and shaping them; synthetic diamonds have had to be produced which are capable of cutting where natural diamonds fail.

The problems of insulation have led Man to experiment with the unlikeliest materials. Fibre-glass and spun-glass have proved excellent for insulation; but glass specially treated and processed has also been found to be excellent for motor-car bodies, racing yachts, ships' lifeboats and anglers' rods. The waste products of coal and petroleum in particular have been found to be a never-ending source of supply of unexpected raw materials. Coal, air and water—three cheap and plentiful ingredients—form the basis of most synthetic plastics, while resins from various sources form the basis for many others.

Plastics form perhaps the most extensive range of examples of Man's inventiveness so far as materials are concerned. Extremely thin, transparent plastics make lightweight waterproofs, curtains and hangings; heavier plastics make 'rubber' sheeting, buckets and bowls and cans and receptacles of every shape and size and use; as perspex—glass-clear, easily moulded, tough and practically

9

unbreakable—it makes heavy sheets for the windows and noses of aircraft; opaque and coloured, flexible but still tough and resistant to wear of every kind, it replaces leather in the upholstery of cars and armchairs. The 'hide', as it may be referred to, started life not on any animal but as calcium carbide!

Man has found a use for practically every so-called waste product that results from the processing of a wide variety of materials in a wide range of industrial activities. Oat husks, soya-bean dust, wood-shavings and sawdust, decayed cereals, worthless scrap fabric, cotton-seed fibre, farm waste generally, and many other substances that until only the other day would have been destroyed as literally worthless, today have their place in industry; hardly a week goes by without some new use being found for something hitherto regarded as useless.

But, exciting as this half-century of inventiveness has been, it is only a fraction of the total time that Man has been on earth and *making* things. He has always been a 'tool-making animal'. This is partly because he has been less generously equipped by Nature with his own built-in tools and partly because his built-in curiosity has always led him to experiment, to try out something that had never been tried out before.

Until, as it were, the day before yesterday, he contented himself with applying his tools to the raw materials that filled the world in which he lived. Readiest to his hand, of course, after the stones and clay with which he built his dwellings, were the naturally growing things: trees, large and small, shrubs of many varieties, reeds and rushes in marshy and well-watered districts, and, when he had learned to sow and reap crops, there was straw.

Timber—whether from the big trees or from the humbler ones—was the first growing material to which he applied his tools. By a process of trial-and-error extending over many generations, many centuries, he discovered which varieties of timber were best suited to his purposes; purposes which grew more numerous and also more complex with every passing year.

Now, here is a remarkable thing. So well suited did a number of these natural materials prove to be for certain purposes that even today, in this highly scientific age of electronics, there are still certain uses where the natural material is preferred to the synthetic. Though craftsmen in factories are gradually being ousted by the miracles of automation, there are still country craftsmen making things today of traditional materials, and making them as they have been made literally for centuries, in established ways that cannot be improved upon, or even equalled, by men operating machines.

It is no exaggeration to say that so long as our soil continues to produce timber, reeds, straw and other natural materials such as these, so long will craftsmen continue to turn these materials to good account while working in the tradition of the craftsmen who lived before them. In the pages which follow we will take a look at some of these traditional craftsmen, the materials they work in, the tools they have evolved to cut and shape the materials, and the skill with which they handle tools and materials in the making of articles that possess beauty combined with usefulness of a kind that machine-made articles rarely possess.

Craftsmen in Willow and Osier

WILLOW, and its offshoot, osier, are probably more widely used by craftsmen in the countries where they grow than any one other natural material: they have as many uses as have been found in the Far East for bamboo—far too many to count.

There are many reasons for the popularity of willow and osier with craftsmen. They grow everywhere in England and in much of Scotland, Wales and Ireland; there are so many varieties that foresters refer to them as the willow 'tribe'; they grow so fast that many varieties are ready for the craftsman's use when only a year old, and they reproduce themselves so rapidly that there is a continuous and inexhaustible supply of them at all times. Most important of all, perhaps, is the fact that osier can be manipulated if necessary without any tools at all, and willow is so adaptable and pliant that it can be worked with the very simplest of tools: it has always been the primitive, or poorly equipped, craftsman's stand-by.

He has used it for literally thousands of years. Archaeologists digging in the ancient peat-beds of Denmark have found relics of many types of basket used by people living there between five and six thousand years ago. Some of these had merely been containers; others had been more elaborately woven into fish-traps. The earth and stones dug from the great ditch behind Hadrian's Roman Wall, that spanned England from the North Sea to Solway, were carried in osier baskets to build the northward-facing rampart. A thousand years ago, when King Offa of Mercia built his famous dyke along the Welsh Border between Chepstow and Prestatyn, the serfs dug earth and stone with ox shoulder-blades and carried it in osier baskets to a westward-facing rampart.

Such baskets, of course, were very roughly constructed, the thick osiers being simply woven or plaited to a handy size. Craftsmen, however, have always been noted for the time and thought they give to improving both the efficiency and the appearance of their products, and so during the fifty centuries and more of basket making the various shapes and patterns have increased and also acquired a better 'finish'.

Originally, the osier was used in its natural state. Osier workers soon found, however, that it not only 'worked' better, but looked better, if it was first peeled. They evolved a simple method of preparing the cut 'rods', and this method is still in use today, after hundreds of years, because no better method has ever been found.

The bundles of cut rods are first stood upright in running water, a process called 'pitting'. Then use is made of a primitive but most efficient tool known as a 'break'. It consists of nothing more than a 'Y'-shaped piece of hoop-iron, filed to a keen edge and stuck upright in a post driven into the ground at a convenient height for the worker—who may be a man, a woman or even a child. Each rod is drawn, thin end foremost, between the 'Y'-shaped blades of the 'break' so that the peel is automatically stripped off and the pure white rod is left. If, as is the case with some types of basket, the osier is required to have that familiar warm brown colour, then the rods and the peel

OSIER 'BREAK'

are thrown into a tank and boiled together for a while. Dog-baskets, for instance, are nearly always made of these dyed osier rods.

Before the basket maker begins to work with the osiers he soaks them to make them pliant. For his work he needs the absolute minimum of equipment. He sits on a 'floorboard', or 'kneeboard', that slopes slightly away from him and, his back wedged firmly against a wall, works at his basket-weaving between his knees. He has a sharp knife to cut or trim the rods, one or two awls, or gimlets, for making holes or for forcing a way between tight basketwork for a handle or strengthening rod, and an iron bar with eyelets in it, which he calls a 'commander' and uses for straightening bent rods.

For the greater part of the time, however, his tools lie beside him and his quick hands are all that is necessary to manipulate the osier, building up the basket to its required size and shape. One reason why blind people take to basket making so readily is that most of it is done by touch and the deft movements of sensitive fingers which can do this sort of work independently of the supervision of the eye.

The basket maker normally starts with the bottom. The uprights, braced by other rods, form what he calls the 'upset', or the 'slath'. Having made his frame, as it were, he then begins to fill in the interstices—a process he refers to as 'randing'—and strengthens the whole fabric by inserting occasional rows of several rods together, which he calls 'slewing'. Finally, when the basket has reached the required height, he finishes it off by bending over the ends of his uprights and weaving them into a strong border that gives both finish and firmness to the whole. With his sharp knife he trims all the osier ends to a finely sloping angle that enables them to be lost in the basket wall.

For certain types of basket very much thinner osiers are required than are produced by the 'break'. To obtain these, the osier worker makes use of one or other of several simple but very efficient tools. He may have a single blade stuck upright in a post,

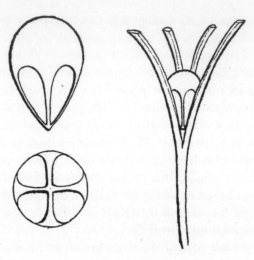

'EGG-SPLIT'

make a nick in each osier rod and then whip it smartly back towards him so that the blade cleaves it straight along the centre. Or he may use his 'egg-split'. This is like a small wooden egg with four grooves carved out of the narrower end. The 'egg' is inserted into the butt-end of each rod and pressed downwards in such a way that the rod is automatically split into four equal quarter segments. Then the thread of pith is removed from each, and the result is a bundle of thin, smooth and supple osier rods known as 'skeins' which can be used for the finer work done by the basket maker.

So many and varied are the osiers he uses for different types of basket that they have acquired a wealth of picturesque names: Russet, Mealy, Long Skins, Light Dicks, Red Root, Black Maul, Mottled Spaniard, Pomeranian, Brittany Green, Dicky Meadows, Champion and Grisette are just a few of these! But even more numerous, of course, are the types of basket that can be woven out of this abundant and most adaptable material.

Among the largest of these are the big rectangular ones used by touring theatrical companies for the transport of their clothes and 'props', and by the laundries handling big quantities of wash-ing. The potato grower uses enormous numbers of heavily constructed potato hampers; Covent Garden porters carry stacks of round bushel and other vegetable and fruit baskets piled high one on the other on their heads and going by names such as 'flats', 'rips', 'pads', 'strikes', 'pots' and 'peck cobs'. There are rectangular baskets for use on tradesmen's bicycles, shopping baskets, cucumber 'flats', basketwork sieves, back-creels used by Scottish fishwives and peat-creels used by workers in Irish bogs; 'crubans', or side-panniers for donkeys, dog-baskets, containers for fragile supplies having to be dropped by parachute, protective baskets for glassware containing chemicals—in fact there is no end to the variety of basket made of osiers thick or thin. There is even a bottomless basket used by potato growers to hold sack mouths open while they are being filled!

But osier has been turned to less usual, and therefore more interesting, articles than baskets such as those just described. For example, wherever crabs and lobsters are to be found, the fisher-men use crab-pots and lobster-pots: ingeniously designed traps into which the slow-moving and dull-witted crustacean blunders and from which it is impossible for him to escape. Experiments have been made with wire netting and similar materials, but it has been found that lobster-pots made of these materials never stand up so well to the chafing of rock and stones and the ground-swell of heavy seas as do those made of the tough, pliant osier, the material traditionally used by all fishermen for the purpose.

There is one curious difference to be seen in this form of basketwork: instead of working on a sloping floorboard and weaving from the board upwards, the lobster-pot maker starts in the middle and works upwards and then downwards! He starts by weaving a narrow funnel about eight or nine inches long. Then he takes his main rods and bends them first outwards like the spokes of a wheel and then downwards. As he does so, he threads more osiers between them, working downwards all the time, till he comes to the final stage.

He then constructs the flat base of the pot, securing it to the circle of rods that first formed the funnel and then continued into the outer circumference of the pot itself. To the base he lashes a heavy stone or two, or a bar or two of iron, to act as ballast, and the necessary ropes and cork floats are then added according to the depth at which the pot is to lie in wait for the lobster or crab. The pot is then complete. It will last the maker, who in all probability is the owner also, for several seasons; and if he is a veteran craftsman it will probably have taken him no more than a couple of hours or so at most to make!

More delicately and ingeniously made than the common crab-pot, however, is the 'eel-grig', which is found in parts of England like the Fens and the Severn Valley where the eel is plentiful. This is a very elaborate, very beautiful example of the craftsman's work in osier. An eel-grig is something like a long, tapering Chinese lantern, but its principle is the same as that of the lobster-pot. It has a cone-shaped entrance which contains a piece of bait to tempt the idly wandering eel; beyond that it has a succession of graduated cones, known to the eel-grig makers as 'inchins', which fit more tightly over their prey than the osiers fit the clumsy lobster, but are made springy, so that having once yielded to admit the eel, they close like a well-fitting door behind him and only open to admit the next victim and those that follow.

Eel-grigs have to be very carefully made to the measurements of the eels frequenting the waters in which they are placed to trap them. The craftsman knows that the eel is cunning, as well as streamlined, and not handicapped as the lobster and crab are handicapped by clumsy claws and other protuberances. More than that, the eel possesses a curious power of self-compression, so the eel-grig maker works with an image of the eel constantly in his mind. He may have a handful of osier gauges by him, against which to measure his 'inchins'; more probably, however, he works by a sort of 'sixth sense' as he weaves each successive cone and fits it into place in the long, tapering trap. It will take him

18

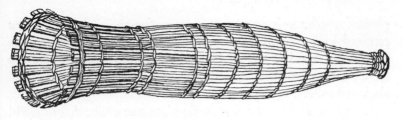

several hours to complete. When he has done, he leaves it to soak in sea water until it has taken on the taste of the water and the scent of his hands has been obliterated. Only then does he go out and place the eel-grig at the spot where he knows, from long observation, the eels congregate. He never forgets that they are cunning and swift-witted and he has to match his wits against theirs.

Other 'specialist' uses for osier include muzzles for calves, carriers for pigeons and other birds, 'cradles' for wine-bottles, garden chairs, and those elaborate beach chairs with hoods and wings to protect the occupant from wind or excessive sunshine, lampshades, and even hats! Not, of course, hats worn by ordinary wearers, though only a hundred years ago very fine osier rods were first plaited together into a 'ribbon', and the ribbon was then wound round and round, its edges sewn together, to make crown and brim of a serviceable lightweight countryman's hat or countrywoman's bonnet. No, today osier is used for the framework of the Guardsman's bearskin, to give it at once the shape, the lightness and the rigidity that are essential.

The osier, however, is the 'poor relation' of the willow, which is a noble tree found usually, though not always, where water is abundant; at least it grows best where the ground is damp and fertile. Most varieties of the 'willow tribe' possess two qualities which it is surprising to find in one type of timber: they are extremely light in weight, yet capable of standing up to severe treatment. For this reason willow is much used for polo balls, which have to be light yet able to withstand the impact of the players' clubs; it is much used, too, for the manufacture of artificial limbs, where lightness is essential because the user has no muscles fitted to the limb, and strength is essential to carry his weight. But there is one use for this timber which stands out above all others: the cricket bat.

The so-called 'cricket-bat willow', a tree evolved by careful training and pruning to yield a straight-grained and practically knot-free timber, is found at its best in Norfolk, Suffolk, Essex and Sussex. It is watched over lovingly in its early years. Every bud on the first eight feet or so of its stem is rubbed away by hand as soon as it appears, so that there shall be no time for a knot to form. When it is about twelve years old it will be nearly five feet in girth at breast height and ready for felling.

Once felled, the willow is cross-cut into lengths of two-foot-eight inches, the standard length for cricket bats. Each of these lengths is then cleft into eight wedge-shaped segments, and each 'cleft', as it is then called, must measure four-and-a-half inches across its outer, curved surface. Though the cross-cut saw may be used for obtaining the lengths of willow from which the clefts will be taken, a saw is never used for obtaining the clefts themselves, for to use a saw would be to risk cutting across the grain and so weakening the timber and making it worthless for a cricket bat or for anything else that had to stand up to hard knocks and wear. Instead, an axe, or a wedge and 'beetle' (or heavy mallet), will be used by the craftsman, who wants his timber to be in perfect condition to work on.

In order to avoid wastage of valuable timber, each 'round' of willow is carefully marked out in radial lines before the actual cleaving is begun. The face of each finished bat will be down a radial line. You can check this for yourself by examining your own bat, when you will find that a succcession of darkish lines, approximately half an inch apart, run the whole length; these are the annual 'growth-rings'.

The clefts are then stripped of their bark, very roughly axe-trimmed to bat shape, and then stacked to season, criss-crossed so that the air can circulate through them, for the better part of a year. They then season indoors for about three months, often in carefully regulated drying-sheds. When this seasoning period is over the timber will have a density of only twenty-one pounds per cubic foot, which makes it lighter than any other British timber, even if it is still not quite so light as balsa wood.

How can a timber that is so soft and easy to work stand up to the impact of a hard ball sent against it by a fast bowler? It is partly because of the resilient quality of the timber itself; partly because of the skill of the craftsman who shapes it to his use. When the blade has been shaped to a somewhat nearer approximation to the finished article, it is passed backwards and forwards between a pair of spring-loaded rollers that exert an increasing pressure upon it until this eventually reaches a figure not far short of two tons to the square inch. The craftsmen turn these rollers by hand when making the best bats, having no faith in mechanically operated rollers that lack the 'feel' which they themselves possess as a result of years of craftsmanship.

'BEETLE' AND WEDGE

Nor is this form of compression the only one they have at their disposal. They use also a specially designed hammer with which, by judicious and steady application, they further compress the fibres of the blade-to-be, as it were kneading them together to increase their toughness and resilience. Only when the texture of the blade is considered satisfactory can it be cut to the exact prescribed length and begin to receive the final proportions which make the difference between a fine bat and a second-rate one.

The craftsman works first with a draw-knife—a two-handled blade which, in the hands of an expert, can cut wafer-thin slivers from a hunk of roughly shaped timber and produce from it a thing of beauty. He also cuts the wedge-shaped slot in the top of the bat to take the 'tooth', or splice of the handle. Now tools must be sharpened to a razor edge; glue must be of the perfect temperature and consistency, cramps adjusted to a nicety, the canes bonded and the rubber inset between them: this is a work of art.

Only when blade and handle have been assembled, however, does the craftsman start on the final stage. A cricket bat is not just a piece of willow of a certain length and cross-section; it must increase in thickness from splice down to the business-end; its weight must be exactly the right one for its length, and the main weight must be in the right part of the blade.

The final shaping is a matter of 'feel' rather than comparison with any form of gauge or template. The craftsman works by eye, but almost more than that he works by a sense of touch, something which he has developed over half a lifetime at his trade. The slope of the shoulders of the bat, the curve on the two edges, the final slope-in at the bottom of the bat, the shape of the curve across the bat at the point where it will rest on the ground while in use: all these are aspects of bat making which only the true craftsman can be certain of fulfilling to perfection.

With draw-knife, and afterwards with a succession of spoke-shaves, each finer than the last, he must trim and peel off slivers of willow, thin perhaps and transparent as tissue-paper, until he has achieved the balance and distribution of weight essential to a fine bat. All the time he is at work he is conscious that, though he can always skim off a wafer-thin shaving, he can never put one back. One cut too many, however fine it may be, and the bat will never be exactly the bat he intended it to be.

No two blades are ever identical—though it may take a real expert to detect any difference between them. Each bat is an individual—like the man who made it. Probably it is with a mixture of relief and regret that the craftsman lays down his draw-knife and spokeshave and hands over the bat to be sanded and burnished and stamped with whatever trademark or cricketer's name has been designed for it: he is relieved that he has completed one more perfect bat; he is loath to let go of a piece of craftsmanship of which he has every reason to be content, even if not proud.

In a way, of course, it is true that cricket-bat making is not just a country craft. Cricket bats are made today in thousands for amateur and professional cricketers the world over. Nevertheless, the making of cricket bats is limited to a fairly small number of centres, in Sussex and Cambridgeshire, Nottinghamshire and parts of Yorkshire, for example. One of the oldest centres is Robertsbridge, in Sussex, where ninety years ago the local carpenter started making bats for himself and a few friends. Then he made bats for W. G. Grace, for 'Ranji', for C. B. Fry and many another great, almost legendary, cricketer. Today it is still possible to see, in a Robertsbridge workshop where bats are made, a letter from the great 'W.G.' telling how with one of that village craftsman's bats he made his hundredth century and scored his thousandth run.

Sussex, too, can claim to be the only county where the 'trug' is made—and trug making is limited to a couple of small villages in the east of that county, Herstmonceux and East Hoathly. This Sussex 'trug' is a link between the osier and the willow, for it is a 'basket' that is made of willow slats which themselves are often 'off-cuts' from cricket-bat making.

This shallow, boat-shaped 'basket' is unique, both in its shape and in the materials of which it is constructed. It is used mainly by fruit growers, farmers and gardeners, and is beautifully adapted (like so many country-made articles) to the purposes for which it was originally designed and is still used. Its odd name, 'trug', may be a corruption of an old word for a shallow boat; certainly its curious flowing shape suggests this. And not only has it a boat-shaped appearance—rather like a small, shallow coracle— but the principle on which it is constructed is that of any clinker-built boat, such as the majority of rowing-boats, in which the 'strakes' run in a continuous swelling line from stem-post to stern.

Two kinds of wood go to the making of the Sussex trug. The frame, and the oval handle which encircles the trug, are made of sweet chestnut; the body is made of thin strips of willow curved and so shaved as to fit closely one over the other.

Chestnut poles are first cleft, much as the smaller osier rods are cleft, on what is called a 'cleaving-frame'. The craftsman uses a 'beetle' and a curiously shaped axe known as a 'fromard', or 'froe'. This has a longish, narrow blade set at right angles to the haft but with the cutting-edge on the lower side. The handle is long enough to enable the worker to force it this way and that while the blade is lightly tapped downwards through the centre of the pole, and the leverage thus obtained enables the pole to be split quite easily. A thick pole will make four 'clefts', a thin one only two.

Each cleft is then shaved smooth on the inner side so that the pith is completely removed, while the thin bark is left on the opposite side. It is then soaked for a short while in a trough of hot water heated by a fire made from shavings and off-cuts, then bent round an oval wooden template and clamped there to 'set', while the overlapping ends are nailed or riveted together. When a pair of these chestnut bands, one large and one small, have set, they are placed at right angles to one another and nailed into position so that they make between them the rim of the trug and the handle by which it is to be carried.

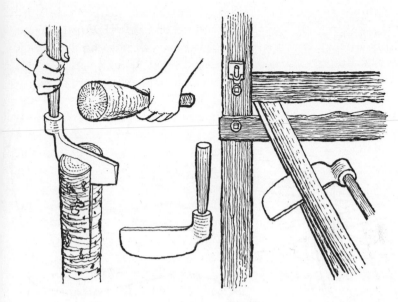

'FROMARD', OR 'FROE'

Meanwhile other workers have been slicing baulks of willow into great numbers of short strips ranging between three and perhaps five inches in width and a little more than an eighth of an inch in thickness. Each worker has a stack of these on the floor beside him as he sits on a low stool in front of his wooden 'horse'. The 'horse' is a much-scarred framework of roughly hewn wood consisting of a thick plank that slopes down towards him and a swivelling 'jaw' that he operates with nothing more elaborate than foot pressure to grip the end of the willow slat he is about to shave to the right dimensions.

Like all good craftsmen, he works by eye and by touch or 'feel'. He has beside him a stack of willow strips, or slats, each of which has to be trimmed to a smooth finish on each side, curved at each end on one side only, and also tapered to a knife-edge on one side. With a swift movement he snaps the end of a strip into the jaw of his 'horse' and hardly is it gripped before he has begun

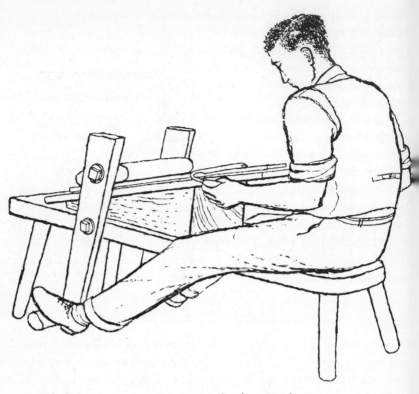

TRUG-MAKER'S 'HORSE'

work with his keen draw-knife. This fines-down the strip to
exactly the right tapering thickness from end to end. As quickly,
he reverses the strip in his simple vice and completes the other
end, then turns it on its edge and with a few deft strokes produces
the right curve first on one end and then on the other. With one
hand he drops the finished strip to the floor, with the other he
picks up the next strip to work on.

He has no pencil-lines to guide him; he uses no foot-rule or
other form of gauge; he hardly even seems to look at what he is
doing. His keen draw-knife appears to operate without guidance

from him at all. Yet it never makes a false stroke, never cuts too deep, never shaves away an iota too much. Steadily one pile decreases and the other pile mounts beside him until there are perhaps a hundred and more willow slats prepared and ready for assembling.

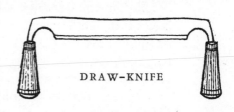

DRAW-KNIFE

Some craftsmen like to complete each trug as they go along; the majority prefer to collect their frames and slats, and then assemble the trugs when they have enough to produce quite a goodly number all at once. But the system of working is basically the same in either case.

First, the 'keel' of the trug, the central, very delicately tapered slat, is laid down, its two ends nailed into the dead centre of the opposite ends of the chestnut rim, and a couple of nails driven

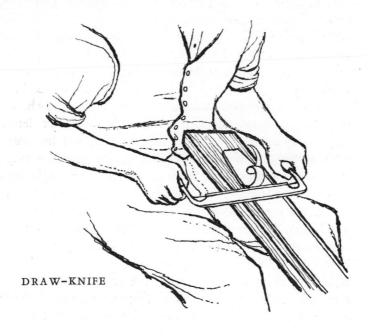

DRAW-KNIFE

through the middle of the slat into the underside of the oval handle which is to surround the finished trug. He then selects, one at a time, the willow slats he has prepared, each one curved and bevelled on one side only, and lays them one on each side of the 'keel'; then another pair one on each side of the first pair; and so on until he reaches the underside of the rim, and the body of the trug is complete. Most trugs consist of seven slats in all, three on each side of the central one.

The fining-down of one edge of each slat makes it possible for the trug maker to fit each one so that it overlaps slightly, without showing any gap and without bulging unduly. Each slat is pressed down until it follows exactly the curve of the one already in position; a nail is driven through into the bottom of the oval supporting the trug, and the two ends of each slat made fast to the inner edge of the rim at each end.

From the side, a trug looks like any clinker-built boat. Its slats fit together as the strakes of a boat fit one another. But looked down on from above, the effect is of a smooth, flattened-curve interior. This is thanks to the skilled tapering and bevelling of one side of each slat to 'bed down' against its neighbour. It remains only to fix two transverse 'legs' beneath the trug and it will stand firm and steady for a long, long time to come.

But the trug maker, like all craftsmen, will not pass his product until he is satisfied that it is perfect. His quick eye detects any unevenness where the frame-ends overlap, and his keen knife whittles this unevenness away. Willow, though soft, is tough, and the end-grain takes some cutting. The amateur might sprain his wrist or forearm, trying to slice through it to obtain a clean finish. The veteran knows how to do this without undue effort. The inside of his knee, set against the outer edge of his right hand, clutching a knife with a keen, curved blade, gives him just the pressure he needs: the overlapping ends of the seven willow slats making up the body of the trug are sliced as cleanly flush with the rim as though they were a part of it; which, indeed, they really are, for the trug of chestnut and willow is a single unit.

It is a fine example of beauty and utility combined. It is at once extremely light and remarkably strong; it is so shaped as to be easy to fill and no less easy to empty at need; it is so balanced that quite heavy weights can be carried without risk of their spilling out. And its curves are such as to give pleasure to the eye, just as the curves of a boat—of any boat—give pleasure by their proportions and their adequacy for the duties for which they have been designed.

Like so many of the rapidly diminishing number of craftsmen-made products, the trug is the result of trial-and-error. It has the shape and proportions that have evolved over the generations during which it has been made in this corner of Sussex. The men who make it are in many cases the sons and grandsons of those who made trugs before them. In some cases the very tools have been handed down from father to son and grandson, for a good tool, carefully treated, has a very long lifetime.

In an age when most manufacturing is done 'against the clock', with time-and-motion-study and automation watching over the factory-hands, the trug continues to be made of the same materials, in the same way, and with the same few basic tools, as it has always been made. Because the trug maker is an expert craftsman, with the feel of his materials and of his simple, efficient tools ingrained in his wrists and fingertips, he can turn out perhaps fifty or sixty or more trugs in a working week, each one as perfect as the one that went before it and the one that will come after it.

Smaller by far than the trug, but very useful in their humble way, are the various types of 'chip' baskets used for containing small quantities of strawberries, raspberries and watercress and so on. Naturally these too are made of willow, because no other wood is so easy to handle with the minimum of tools, and therefore so cheap and simple to produce.

The willow strips of which these 'chips', or 'punnets', are made are almost paper-thin. They are obtained by cleaving willow poles along their annual rings so that long, thin, pliant strips are produced that can be 'woven' as easily as ribbon.

Cottage craftsmen in the West Country, and gipsies travelling the Cotswolds, used to make enormous quantities of these 'baskets', children working even faster than their parents.

Only a very simple tool was necessary for producing these ribbons of willow. It consisted of a sort of comb with two teeth, made out of a piece of hoop-iron filed to a sharp edge like that of the 'Y'-shaped 'break' used by the osier workers. Through it the punnet makers drew long strips of willow so that they were reduced to a uniform width of about an inch. These willow ribbons were quickly woven criss-cross into the standard chip or punnet to hold half a pound or a pound of soft fruit or a lesser quantity of cress. Today, since travelling gipsies cannot supply the demand for punnets, whole logs of willow are rotated against sharp knives until a paper-thin 'veneer' of willow many feet, or even yards, in length is obtained. But then the craftsman takes over and, adopting the traditional methods, cuts his sheet into ribbons, and weaves his ribbons into the finished punnet. It has, like the Sussex trug, remarkable strength in proportion to its lightness and no better container for soft fruit has yet been devised, even in this age of plastics!

Perhaps most housewives today like best the brightly coloured plastic clothes-pegs, but there are still a great many, especially in the country districts, who remain faithful to the simple, old-fashioned willow peg; and the willow peg has always been associated with the travelling gipsy. There is still a good chance, therefore, that in any gipsy encampment that is reasonably near to where willow grows you will see a family sitting round the steps of the caravan hard at work on peg-making.

The clothes-peg is usually made of the poorest type of willow, known as the goat-willow, or sallow, which tends to grow on rough and swampy ground and is useless for other purposes. The gipsy knows this, and you will often find he has pitched camp near a coppice of this scrub willow to save himself trouble and time in search.

The gipsy picks a few lengths, the best he can find, strips off the thin bark and cuts them up into the right length for peg making—a matter of perhaps four inches or so. The thinner stems will be all right for his purpose as they are; the thicker ones may have to be cleft into two, three or even four segments and then trimmed till they are more or less round.

While he has been travelling along the road his keen eyes have been on the alert for any tins that may have been thrown into ditch or hedge-bottom. Any that he spies he immediately salvages: there will be some use for it before long, as he well knows! If he is a peg maker, he knows that use in advance. One of his few tools is a cherished pair of metal-cutters. With these he cuts from his salvaged tins as many narrow strips, perhaps a quarter-inch in width, as he can obtain from them. Deftly he binds one of these strips round a piece of willow about half an inch or so from one end, and taps a nail into it to hold it in place.

He then up-ends the piece of willow, with the tin-bound end downwards, and splits it down the middle with a light, accurate blow of his wood-chopper, or his heavy knife. Then, with a few brisk cuts, he trims away a little wood on the inside of each half of the cleft peg, smooths it so that it will not catch in the threads of any garment it pegs to the housewives' lines, and the peg is complete.

He makes a dozen, two dozen, half a gross, a gross or more, with his wife and family helping him; then his daughters go off to the nearest village or town to sell them, perhaps clipped together on a strip of willow bark a dozen at a time. They are cheaper than the brightly coloured plastic kind, but even at that they have cost the gipsy nothing at all, for the raw materials—the goat-willow and the discarded tin—were there for the taking, and he and his family had all the time in the world. His 'profit' is 100 per cent, and the housewife has got an article which cost her very little and may well outlast any shop-bought clothes-peg however novel or expensively produced!

You will look, though, at a thousand such clothes-pegs and you will never find one that has been *sawn*; they are always *cleft*.

Willow must be cleft—whether for basket making, cricket-bat making, trug making or clothes-peg making: down the grain there is strength and resilience; across it—weakness and death.

One very curious use of willow existed in this country for more than eight centuries after the Norman Conquest. This was the use of the willow 'tally stick', as a form of 'receipt' for money paid. Grooves representing pounds, shillings and pence were cut round the stick. Then the stick was cleft—not sawn: this was very important. One half of the cleft stick was retained by one party, the other half by the other party.

It was important that the two halves should be retained, for if either half was lost, the other party could protest that payment had not been made, or had been made and not 'receipted'. It would be possible to forge grooves and other marks, if one half were to be lost; but no one could forge the grain of the wood; this is why the stick had always to be cleft, not sawn. In fact, the very word 'tally' comes from the Norman-French word *tailler*, meaning 'to cleave'.

Incidentally this curious practice gave our language a saying that we often use though we may never stop to think what it really means. When we say 'He's the spit and image of his father', for instance, we are really saying in our own way 'splitten image': this was the cleft, or 'split', wood, both halves of which, when brought together, showed an exact likeness!

The past life, and usefulness, of willow and osier are long; its life and usefulness in the future may well be just as long or longer. For here is a natural raw material abundantly growing, simple to 'work', attractive when handled by craftsmen, and possessing qualities for which our age of inventiveness has not yet found a really satisfactory substitute.

Craftsmen in Oak

IT WOULD be hard to find any timber offering a greater con-
trast to the soft, pliant, easily worked willow than the oak
tree does. Oak is hard, tough, enduring. We think of it as a
typically British tree—though it is found also in countries as
distant as Japan. We talk of 'English oak' when we want to pay
tribute to the sterling qualities of something, or even of someone.
The words 'heart of oak' are a tradition in the Navy and where-
ever the qualities of courage, toughness and endurance need to be
described.

Take its powers of endurance first. Some years ago dredgers
working on the Thames laid bare a system of stakes which the
experts believe were driven into the river bed as a defence against
the Romans under Julius Caesar—almost two thousand years
ago! But oak has lasted even longer than that: primitive canoes,
dating from prehistoric times, have been excavated from Thames
mud near Windsor. The lasting qualities of oak were taken into
account by the builders of a small Essex church a thousand years
ago, and though some of the great baulks of oak have now rotted
at the point where they stick out of the ground in which they
were set, in the main they are strong and sturdy after ten centuries.
Oak piles were used as foundations when the cathedral at
Winchester was built, some nine hundred years ago, and they
have been found to be in good condition still.

Even salt water is unable to destroy the lasting powers of this
fine timber, which is indeed practically indestructible. An oak-
built sailing ship, the *Mary Rose*, was recently salvaged. She had

foundered nearly half a century before the coming of the Spanish Armada, but when she was examined her massive oak timbers were still sound! Because oak has this power of resistance to the action of sea water it is much used in harbour works. The harbour at Gibraltar was constructed of oak baulks from the forests of Dorset, and when the Suez Canal was under construction oak baulks were brought all the way from the great oak forests of Atholl, in Scotland. Man turns to oak whenever he requires a timber that can be guaranteed to last practically for ever.

It is not only long lasting, it is hard; and, unlike many other timbers, which tend to lose their strength with the passing of time, oak hardens with age. Try to drive a nail into an old oak beam and you will find that the nail will almost always bend over before it has penetrated more than a fraction of an inch. Try to turn a screw into the beam: it will be gripped as in a vice after a couple of turns, and if you persist you will screw its head off altogether. You can use the phrase 'hard as oak' just as well as 'hard as nails', especially if you are referring to oak several hundred years old.

The size of the oak-tree has always been remarkable: not so much its height as the bulk of its trunk and main boughs and the great spread of its branches. Wherever you see a really outstandingly large tree, the chances are that it will be an oak. Many of them are so gigantic that they have been given names: the Major Oak, for instance, in Sherwood Forest, or the Knightwood Oak, in the New Forest. The famous Boscobel Oak became a part of our history when it sheltered Charles II three centuries ago. Largest of them all is the famous Newlands Oak, in the Forest of Dean. Its girth at breast height—the height at which tree measuring is ordinarily done—is forty-four feet: this means a diameter of over fourteen feet. And since it is now a hollow shell, you could put inside it a large dining-table and set a dozen or more people round it!

One of the earliest constructional uses to which the oak was

OAK 'KRUCKS'

put was the building of houses of 'wattle-and-daub' fitted into a massive timber framework. If you look carefully at any of these very ancient buildings—there are some good examples in many small villages in districts where there have long been oak forests —you will find that each end of the building consists of two enormous timbers slanting upwards and inwards to meet at the end of the roof ridge. Look very carefully at these timbers, and you will usually find that they are a matching pair. They will probably not be straight; they may have a slight 'knee' part way up their length; but if so, the two 'knees' will correspond to one another.

These matching pairs of timbers are called 'krucks', and the principle of building is known as 'kruck'-construction. The old-time builders went to the nearest oak forest and looked out for a suitable tree, or major bough of a tree, and felled it. Using giant wedges, the men cleft the baulk of timber from end to end so as

35

to obtain two exact halves. It might have been quicker to rip-saw them, but that would have meant risking a cut across part of the grain and thereby losing the necessary strength and endurance. The matching halves were then erected on the proposed site, slanting inwards from what would be the outer walls to meet, like a pair of whale jaws, two storeys overhead and be firmly pinned together with oak pins as thick as your arm.

A similar pair of krucks would be erected some distance away, according to the size of the building planned; their two tips would be joined with a ridge pole, and the sides and ends of the framework completed by a criss-cross pattern of stout oak beams running horizontally and vertically. The spaces in between would then be filled in with big panels of wattle-and-daub. You can see this form of construction in many of the giant barns and farm buildings up and down the country, particularly in such counties as Herefordshire, Worcestershire and Gloucestershire, which were fortunate in having the very ancient Forest of Dean with its mighty oak-trees almost on their doorstep. Those oak krucks and other timbers, which have withstood wind and weather for centuries, are hard as iron: you cannot drive a penknife blade into them however sharp it is. And they are most of them likely to stand up for as long again as they have done already.

The early shipbuilders, of course, turned to oak as soon as they began to build on a large scale. There is something in common between the building of the frames of the old 'Wooden Walls' and those of the kruck houses and barns. Stem-post and stern-post were the vital parts of the framework and were always made of oak. In vessels such as those in which Nelson's men sailed, these posts might be anything up to forty feet in length and thirty inches thick even at their smaller ends. Because of the need for perfect timber for these very purposes, oaks were planted and watched over by successive generations of shipwrights so that they would always have a supply of suitable trees waiting for them.

For stem and stern, straight, or very slightly curved, timber was necessary. But the shipwrights' needs did not finish there. They required oak for the 'ribs' and for the 'knees'—the angular joints that locked the cross-shelves, or deck-joists, to the sloping ribs. Timber shaped by sawing would not be strong enough for these; it was necessary to find, or actually to grow, timber that would have approximately the right shape before it was hewn down. The ribs would all be curved, and the curves would change as the sides of the ship swelled from stem-post to its maximum beam, and inwards again to the blunt stern. The knees would all be bent, the angles varying with the position of each successive pair.

So, the shipwright saw to it that oak-trees were grown in two ways. Some were planted close together, so that their trunks soared upwards, without any branches, in an attempt to reach the sunshine and open air. From these great oaks came the stem-posts and stern-posts. Other oaks were planted wider apart and their stems were cut back while they were still young. This caused the oaks to 'coppice'—to throw out new stems in all directions and often of fantastic shapes. From these, the ship-wright-craftsman selected his ribs and knees.

Just as, today, iron- and steelworks and other heavy industries tend to be situated within easy reach of good supplies of coal, so the most notable shipyards used to be sited as near as possible to the best oak forests. At Buckler's Hard, in Hampshire, the ship-wrights worked in oak floated down the Beaulieu from the New Forest; Porstmouth shipwrights used oak from the ancient Forest of Bere; Severn Estuary shipwrights relied on oak from the Forest of Dean; Merseyside shipwrights relied on the ancient Forest of Delamere; Chatham shipwrights used oak from the great forests of the Kentish Weald; and so on.

But these are craftsmen working on the grand scale, building houses and ships of English oak. The timber served other, and humbler, purposes as well. The first spades to be used after man had started looking for something more serviceable than ox shoulder-blades were carved out of oak, sometimes reinforced with a strip of iron along the cutting-edge. Oak spades have been dug out of bogland in the Lake District and are known to be some two thousand years old. Long before the plough was used in this country, the craftsman-farmer used a 'hack', an oak branch with a strong fork in it, which served him as something midway between a spade and a mattock.

When agriculture became properly established and farmers built up extensive farms, it was to oak that they looked for their gateposts and railings; it is still the first choice, if the farmer can afford the price, for these purposes. If you see a gatepost being installed, you will find that though it has been expertly square-cut and trimmed to an angle at the top to throw off the rain, the part that is to go beneath the ground is a massive, unhewn butt like the main root of the tree itself. Well embedded, an oak gatepost will last indefinitely and never warp or sag, however heavy the gate that it carries.

Oak has a splendid grain, and from earliest times craftsmen working in it have known that it is better cleft than sawn. It must always be split 'the way of the grain', otherwise its finest qualities, of toughness and sheer strength, will have been taken from it. But because oak grows to such great proportions, the craftsman working in this timber has had to devise various methods of cleaving it.

Very big butts have to be split with what he calls an 'explosive wedge'. This is a smallish, hollow wedge into which he packs a charge of blasting powder. It is tapped lightly into the exact centre of the butt-end and then a slow-burning fuse is set off. The explosion will split the butt into two or more segments, which can then be trimmed by the craftsman with his axe or other tools.

Oak less bulky he can split with wedges and the heavy mallet he calls a 'beetle', or 'biddle', or 'maul'. The wedge is a heavy, tapering slab of iron with a groove running down the middle of each side which helps to keep it straight when it is being driven home and also makes it easier to extract. The mallet, whatever name it carries, is a tool with a heavy head, of oak or elm or other hard wood on to which the blacksmith has shrunk two iron bands to prevent it from splitting, and a long, straight handle, usually of ash.

With three wedges and a beetle a woodman can reduce a heavy baulk of solid oak to a number of equally proportioned segments in a very short time indeed. His accurate eye and sense of judgment, a pair of arms and hands working in exact conjunction: these enable him to make a thing of use and often even of beauty out of a tough and unmanageable-looking twelve-foot butt of oak a yard or so in diameter and looking, to the inexpert eye, absolutely invulnerable.

It is out of cleft oak such as this that the craftsman makes the best gates and rails—both the short uprights, known as 'piles', 'stiles' or 'stobs', and the longer horizontals. If you examine a length of railings on the boundary, or round the stackyard, of a well-found farm, you will find that they have been very skilfully assembled, in a tradition the craftsman has practised all his life, like his father and grandfather before him.

Each upright has had two or more slots, or mortises, cut into it, the uppermost one not less than five inches from the top. The rails themselves are usually nine feet long and each end is tapered. The men who erect this type of fencing have to work a stage at a time, because since each tapered end has to bed down with the taper on the preceding length it always has to be inserted before the upright is finally driven home. In this way the two matching rail ends lock together, completely filling the mortise, and there is no need for nailing them because they are now jammed tight. Once in, the tenons occupy the whole of the mortises and the fence becomes a single unit; and so durable is the timber of which it has been made that it will last for fifty years or more without attention.

The best farm gates are always made of cleft oak. Inferior ones are made of sawn oak, and you hardly need to approach them to notice the difference. A cleft-oak gate is a work of art, the product of a craftsman whose whole life has been devoted to making such things in a tradition that has been proved sound. It has refinements that no factory-produced, sawn-oak gate is likely to possess. For example, the upright to which the hinges are attached, known as the 'harr', is much heavier than the opposite side, which carries the latch; the top rail is beautifully tapered off from the 'harr' end to the opposite end, for the strain, as the craftsman well knows, comes at the hinge, and weight can, and should, be spared at the end which swings free.

The mortises, too, are expertly cut. The ends of the rails, whether the heavier top rail or the lighter rails that make up the 'five-barred gate', fit perfectly into these mortises—a fit that is snug and tight, reinforced, perhaps, by an oak peg fashioned by the craftsman himself and driven home with a tap of his mallet to weld the two parts, horizontal and vertical, into one unit.

Oak pegs have always been favourites with craftsmen, and for many purposes are much more satisfactory than even the best square-cut nails. A small oak peg, fashioned by a craftsman and possessing exactly the right degree of taper, will lock mortise and tenon together as firmly, and endure as long, as any nail. The shipwrights who built our 'Wooden Walls' used oak pegs not only to fasten knees to ribs but to fasten keels to stem-posts and stern-posts—enormous pegs like truncheons that hardened with age and stood up to the friction of movement and to the effects of salt water and wind and sun better than any iron bolts could do. Carpenters building kruck-type houses locked the massive framework together with oak pegs an inch and more thick. You can see the ends of these projecting from the timbers today, and even the end-grain is so hard that if you stab at it with a penknife you will make no more impression on it than if you had used your fingernail! Even today, millions of oak pegs are used to pin down the 'chairs' on the sleepers of our railway system.

Another example of the art of the craftsman working in oak is a type of light fencing known as 'cleft oak pale'. It consists of slats of cleft oak about a quarter of an inch thick standing upright against an oak frame, each slat overlapping a fraction with the one next to it, and secured to it by a galvanized-iron nail. The effect is much like that of the strakes of a clinker-built boat, though of course the slats are vertical and straight.

To obtain these slats, the craftsman first cleaves his bole of oak, as though for a gatepost or heavy rail. But when he has his segments, he turns to a new tool which closely resembles the trug-maker's 'fromard'. This is his 'froe'. It has the same shortish, straight handle and long, narrow blade sharpened on the lower edge. Holding his froe in his left hand, he taps it firmly with his mallet, the edge of the blade being inserted into the end-grain of the oak. Easing his blade steadily downward by a levering motion of the handle while he taps with his mallet, he gradually produces from each segment of oak a number of long, thin slats, cleft in such a way that the grain is not once broken and also so that each slat is fractionally wider on one side than on the other. This is highly skilled work, calling for a keen eye and accurate judgment.

Cleft oak pale fencing is often erected so that each panel, perhaps eight or nine feet long and six feet high, alternates with the ones adjoining it, the edges showing first on the one, the flats showing first on the next, and so on. It is this arrangement that causes the regularly alternating sound that you can hear in the echo such a fence throws back when a car goes past. Such fencing is a pale golden brown when it is first erected, but the effect of weathering is to give it a pale silvery-grey hue in which the beautiful grain stands out like a watermark in expensive paper.

Houses, ships, gates and fences: these are three widespread uses for oak in which durability as well as strength is of prime importance. But these outstanding qualities make oak invaluable also for much smaller articles that come from the craftsman's bench and workshop.

The wheelwright, for instance, uses oak for the spokes of his cart and waggon wheels, for it is the spoke that takes the heaviest hammering from whatever surface the wheel passes over. The whole weight of the vehicle, or the upward 'thrust' of the road, whichever way you look at it, is momentarily taken by each spoke in turn as it reaches a point vertical to the surface. No timber except oak is strong enough to withstand the incessant hammering a wheel receives. The wheelwrights who made the gun-carriages in the days when army cannon were horse-drawn went on using oak for their spokes long after the use of iron for them had become a practical proposition. Even George Stephenson's 'Rocket' had spokes of oak in its driving-wheels!

As always, the oak a wheelwright uses must be cleft. It must be 'heart of oak', too, if possible—the dead centre of the tree, where the grain is strongest and straightest. 'Cleft heart-wood, the grain unbroken', the wheelwright stipulates when he orders from the timber merchant for this purpose.

It will be the hardest part of the timber. And this is important because the two ends of each spoke must be driven tightly home into the ash 'felloe' and the elm 'stock', or hub, respectively. A wheel must always be what is called 'unsprung weight', and there is therefore nothing to cushion the spoke-end against the continuously repeated shock of impact. Unless the end of the spoke has been driven in so tightly that it becomes one with the timber into which it has been driven, it will eventually work loose and the wheel will lose its strength and trueness. Oak, then, for the spokes, cleft carefully from the heart of the tree or bough from which it is taken.

Having made sure that he has genuine heart-wood, the wheelwright proceeds to fine-down his spokes to the appropriate thickness and proportions. If you examine a waggon wheel closely you will see that a cross-section of a spoke is more or less that of a slightly flattened egg, with the thinner end of the egg facing outwards. That of a spoke fitted to the wheel of a light trap or gig will be much thinner, if longer, and the cross-section much more 'refined'. The shaping of the spoke, whether for a heavy waggon or for a lightweight gig, is done with two tools, the draw-knife and the spokeshave. The first gives the spoke a rough shape, the second trims it to its exactly prescribed proportions—which in the case of the long, thin spoke may be very delicate indeed.

The spokes are first all cut exactly to length. The tenon is cut at each end of the spoke, one of them perhaps being round, the other being rectangular. The 'shoulder' is squared off, to take the strain of pressure when the weight of the vehicle tends to force rim and stock together. Any wood that can be trimmed away without impairing the strength of the spoke is carefully calculated

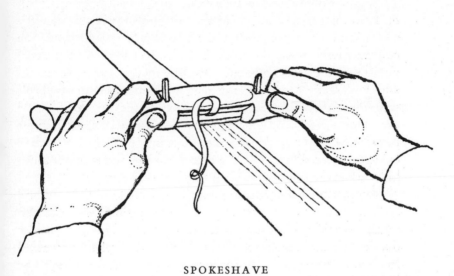

SPOKESHAVE

and removed with deft strokes of the spokeshave. The wheelwright knows that, since a wheel is 'unsprung weight', every pound, every ounce, that can be saved will help the horse that has to work between the shafts. 'Streamlining', too, will not only improve the look of the wheel but help to give it balance as it turns.

This becomes particularly important when he is making wheels for lightweight pony-traps. Each wheel may have as many as sixteen long, thin spokes; every one of them must weigh exactly the same as every other one, to a fraction of an ounce, or the tall, thin, spidery wheel will not run true. But the expert wheelwright works almost without measuring equipment. Once he has cut his spokes to the same length, and scribed-off his tenons and shoulders, he does the rest of his work almost entirely by eye and by the touch of his sensitive fingers. He *feels* what he is doing, as the eel-grig maker feels the tension of the 'inchins' that are taking shape beneath his fingers.

Some of the wheels to be seen on coaches and gigs and even on farm carts and waggons in various museums in this country and abroad are so exquisitely made that you would think the craftsmen who made them worked for sheer love of their craft, rather than for a weekly wage. Wealthy owners of coaches could afford to employ the finest craftsmen in the ancient craft of wheel-wrighting; if they knew the reputation of the man they could give him a free hand and tell him to design the finest, most beautiful wheel he could imagine. They may be looked at today: evidence of the skill and loving care that a true craftsman put into his work every hour of the day, year in, year out.

Another small and commonplace article, not unlike the wheel spoke, that can never be made as well by machinery as it can be by the hand of a craftsman is the ladder rung. Though a ladder does not have to stand up to the same stresses as a wheel, neverthe-less it must be strong in proportion to its weight, for it has to be lifted by muscular power into position and then carry the weight of a man, perhaps two men at a time.

A ladder maker always uses oak for his rungs, and heart of oak if it is to be a top-grade ladder. Sometimes he buys up old cartwheels and breaks them up to obtain the heart-wood spokes, which he will fine-down into ladder rungs, or 'staves', or 'rounds'. These are always very slightly barrel shaped: thick in the middle, and tapered off towards each end in a curving, not a straight, taper.

More often, however, he works from newly cleft and well-

44

'STAVE-BLOCK'

seasoned oak segments. Each segment, having been cleft, is triangular in section, so his first task is to square it by trimming away the sharp corners and bringing it to a uniform thickness very slightly greater than the bulge of the finished spoke.

He works, like the trug maker, in front of a 'horse', though the ladder maker refers to this as his 'break'. It is on the same principle: a swivelling jaw that can be locked down on to the main plank by the pressure of his feet, with the wood he is working on securely gripped by the pressure. The first tool he uses is the draw-knife, with which he rapidly reduces the four corners until he has a near-round bar of oak, still slightly larger than the finished rung is to be. Next he uses a 'stave-block', which is a clumsy-looking but very efficient tool, something like an out-size pencil-sharpener, but containing two sharp, concave-curved blades set opposite one another. With this he obtains his regular rounded taper, working towards each end of the rung in turn, from the centre. The two ends, which have to be set firmly into the ash or spruce ladder sides, are shaped by tapping them into a circular metal gauge with its upper edge sharpened so that each rung is finished off to exactly the same diameter.

Oak is the first choice of the cooper, or barrel maker, too—a craftsman whose skill is second to none among those who work in various timbers. He uses only the very finest-quality oak, and prefers timber from trees that are about two hundred years old, which he judges accurately enough by measuring their girth at breast height. This should be approximately nine to ten feet, which means a diameter of about one yard.

The oak trunk is first cross-cut into the length necessary for the barrel that is to be made, with a slight margin for waste during the process of trimming and shaping. Then, with wedge and maul, the lengths are cleft into segments, each one, of course, being triangular in section, with a fine edge at the heart and the rough bark on its curved outer side. The thin knife-edge, the bark and a certain amount of the sapwood, which comes immediately beneath the bark, is next trimmed away and the barrel maker then measures out the trimmed segment to see how many staves he can obtain from it.

In the case of barrel staves, the clefts are made down the radial lines of the timber. This ensures that each stave contains at least one of what are known as the oak's 'medullary rays', and this in turn ensures that the staves will be watertight—proof against leakage of any liquid, whether wine, cider, beer or spirits. The barrel maker will obtain two, or possibly three, staves from each radial cleft; each of them will be three, four, five or even six inches or more wide, according to the girth of the tree from which they are cut, and anything up to an inch or more in thickness, according to the size of the barrel to be made.

Wedge and maul are sufficient for splitting the oak bole into segments, but something capable of more delicate work is necessary for the staves themselves. Once again, the froe, or fromard, is called into play. Gently but firmly tapping the blunt edge of the blade downwards, so that the keen edge ahead of it penetrates the grain further and further with each tap, and at the same time working the tool lever-wise, with a deft movement of his powerful wrist, the craftsman gradually obtains his staves, one after the other, each the right width and thickness, the grain unbroken from top to bottom; and by the time he has finished his massive baulk of oak has been reduced to a pile containing perhaps several score of oak planks of even thickness, length and width throughout.

This, however, is only the first, and certainly the simplest, stage in the process of barrel making. A barrel may be anything from a little one that you can pick up and tuck under your arm to a giant that needs a pair-horse waggon or a lorry to transport it. But whether small or large, the principle on which it is constructed remains the same. It consists of a large number of oak staves, curved in such a way that when they are bound together

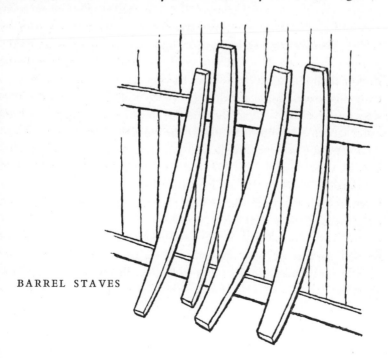

BARREL STAVES

by a number of iron hoops they make a circular container, bulging at the 'equator' and tapering off to two blunt ends, not in a straight line, however, but with the gentlest of graduated curves.

Consider for a moment, then, the problems that confront the barrel maker. He has a pile of oak staves, equal in width throughout their length—which may be six feet or more in the case of the giant barrels. Every one of these has got to be shaped individually in such a way that when they are assembled—and this is one of the most fascinating processes in the work of the barrel maker—they will make a barrel of the right shape, proportions and strength, and moreover one that is absolutely fluid-tight. There will not be a single straight line in any direction in any one of the staves, when he has completed their fashioning, so that the carpenter's stand-by—the ruler and the square—will not be of the slightest use to him.

If you ever have an opportunity to look closely at a barrel stave, perhaps in some junk-yard where the iron hoops have rusted away and the barrel they contained has collapsed into a tangle of staves, examine it carefully. You will see that every stave is slightly curved, like a bow, from end to end; it is also very slightly concave on the inner side, and convex on the outer side, at right angles to its length; it is also considerably wider in the middle than it is at each end, and the line from its bulge to its two ends is an exceedingly gradual curve; in addition to this, the two sides are bevelled to an angle which is slightly acute on the curved outer face and slightly obtuse on the curved inner face.

Every one of these bevelled edges, these gentle curves, whether convex or concave, will be true to the thickness of a piece of tissue paper throughout its length, otherwise the seam between stave and stave would not be fluid-tight. In addition, at each end of each stave there will be a groove cut deep into it to hold the barrel head when the barrel is assembled; and the last inch or so will be further bevelled-off, outwards, according to an old tradition of barrel makers, to give 'finish' to the completed article.

48

If ever there was an example of a craftsman working by eye and touch and feel rather than by rule and gauge, it is the cooper. Because he is working with oak, he needs considerable strength in his fingers and wrists—more so than the worker in willow by a long way. But because he is shaping his material so curiously, he needs a delicate, sensitive touch that is instantly responsive to the accuracy of judgment of his practised eye. The subtle inner and outer curves, the fine angles of his bevelled edges, the calculated long, bow-like curves over the full length of his staves: these must be judged by the craftsman's sixth sense, and will be perfectly attained only after years of concentrated application to his craft, based perhaps on several generations of inherited skill.

His tools are those that we have already seen in use: the mallet and wedge, the froe or fromard, and the draw-knife. But he cannot obtain his curves with one draw-knife alone. In addition to the straight blade, which suffices the trug maker and other craftsmen, he requires a selection of draw-knives with curved blades—some curved for shaping the outer side of the staves, some for shaping the inner sides; some for the broad middle of each stave, some for its tapered ends. The skill required to keep such delicately shaped steel blades in perfect condition, and with a cutting-edge that will trim oak as easily as the trug maker trims willow slats, is of a very high order indeed.

In addition to these tools, however, the barrel maker uses what he calls his 'jointer'. This is a very curious type of plane; a plane with a difference. It is more than six feet in length and is permanently fixed at a slope roughly level with his knee, and with its keen blade facing upwards. Unlike the carpenter's plane, which he holds in his hands and runs backwards and forwards over the wood on his bench, this plane remains rigid, and the barrel maker runs his staves over the upturned blade. So accurate is his eye, and so steady and consistent the pressure he exerts on the wood in his hands, that the stave gradually acquires a perfectly even bevel along first one side and then the other, from bulging middle to tapering ends. As the craftsman slides the stave forwards

BARREL MAKER'S 'JOINTER'

over the cutting-edge, a fine curling ribbon of oak wood is skimmed from it, to rise in a spiral and then drop to the heap already accumulating on the workshop floor.

The assembling of the staves is a work of art. The first stage is referred to as the 'setting-up': the staves are grouped round one of the heavy oak discs that form the two ends of the barrel and a 'truss hoop' is put round their lower ends to hold them lightly but firmly in position. They bulge outwards to their midway point, and then inwards again, the bulge having been produced by steaming them or heating them carefully over a fire of oak chips lit beneath them. During this initial stage they look not unlike the uprights of the osier worker's basket before the 'randing' and 'slewing' operations have been begun.

Then the upper ends of the staves are drawn together. This is done by dropping a noose of rope over them and pulling it progressively tighter and tighter until they are close enough together to take an iron hoop similar to the 'truss-hoop' but more carefully and strongly made. This, of course, is only the first of a series of such hoops that will knit the staves together and complete the barrel. The hoops themselves are craftsmen-made, as you will soon see if you examine one closely. It is not just a ring of hoop-iron, but fashioned to fit the curve and taper of the barrel, so that its circumference on one edge must be slightly greater than that on the other edge. It has been made to measure, and strongly riveted, so that when finally in place it will be in exactly the right position relative to the length of the barrel and the position of the other hoops, and furthermore will be exerting the exactly right degree of compression on the staves it contains.

The barrel maker has to work at great speed when he is fitting the hoops on to the barrel. They are hot when he takes hold of them, and each one must be driven on to the barrel quickly so that it is in position before it has cooled and shrunk on. The craftsman works with a heavy hammer and a tool known as a 'drift'—a metal block something like a wedge that is used to force the hoop downwards against the swell of the barrel. He works his way rapidly round the circumference of the barrel, tapping his drift against the edge of the hoop a few inches further round each time, so that the hoop slides uniformly and settles into position exactly across the grain. Two hoops are set in position a little bit away from the 'equator', or widest bulge of the barrel; other, and smaller, hoops bind the staves together at predetermined points nearer to the two heads of the barrel, the last ones not being finally driven home until the oak disc has been inserted into its grooves and 'caulked' so that the finished barrel shall be absolutely fluid-tight.

A barrel possesses enormous strength. The fact that it is curved in all directions means that it can withstand very heavy shocks—when it is dropped to the ground, for instance, during off-loading. And long after it has ceased to be used by the wine merchant or distiller, perhaps because the oak is deemed to be too much impregnated with alcohol for his present purposes, it retains a useful life as a support for heavy weights in builders' and car-breakers' yards and garages, where strength and solidity combined with ease of handling are important.

The cooper's main trade may be in the production of barrels and casks for wine, beer and spirits; but there are many other calls, too, on his skill and expertise. Fish is stored and transported in great quantities in big fish markets such as Grimsby, Hull and Billingsgate, and the barrels in use there, though they do not have to be absolutely watertight, must be very strongly made to stand up to the hard wear and tear of the fish porters and trawler men. Barrels are much used in the bigger cheese-producing districts, such as Cheshire; when butter making was carried on at almost every dairy farm, the churns were the work of the cooper; tubs, bins, oak pails—called 'noggins' or 'piggins' in Ireland and elsewhere—were products of the cooper's craft; harvesters in olden times, and sometimes even today, carry their liquid refreshment out into the fields in miniature barrels, beautifully made, that are exact replicas of the barrels and casks and vats that the cooper has made for centuries past.

Though the great merit of oak is its strength and endurance, which make it more suitable than any other timber for big construction jobs such as harbour works, houses, windmills, and, formerly, ships, oak possesses other qualities, too. If the craftsman working in a big way demands oak two hundred or more years old, there are craftsmen also who select scrub oak and young oak for purposes that are humbler but, in their way, hardly less necessary to the lives of country folk.

Young oak stems are pliant, even if not as pliant as willow or hazel or ash. They are also comparatively easily 'worked'—an important feature in the eyes of the country craftsman whose tools may be few and simple. So they are much used in certain districts for containers that need to be stronger than they would be if the slighter willow, hazel or ash were to be used. One of these is the 'spelk', an oval basket-like container known also as a 'swill', a 'slop', a 'skip' or a 'whisket', and found chiefly in the Furness region of North Lancashire.

The spelk is used for the transport of small quantities of coal; potato growers make good use of it, because it is strong enough to contain a big load of potatoes and the heavy, damp soil which clings to them when they have been dug up; among the Lancashire cotton mills the spelk was once almost universally used for carrying the heavy wooden bobbins and the loads of cotton-waste from one part of the mill to another; cockle fishers on the extensive Lancashire sands have found the spelk ideal for their purposes; farmers in the North Country have used the spelk, rather specially shaped for their purposes and known as a 'kidney-lip' or 'side-slop', when they have been hand-sowing their seed. There are many other similar uses for this very strong and durable basket.

The spelk maker works entirely with young, or scrub, oak, and with the simplest of tools. The saplings are cleft, not sawn (except that they are of course cross-cut for length), but he refers to this by the word 'rent'. Because the wood is soft, and the diameter of a sapling very slight, it can be torn asunder and there is no need for beetle and wedge or even for fromard or froe. A sharp knife, an odd little tool something like the 'egg-split' of the osier worker, consisting of three short blades set at an angle to one another, and a stake driven firmly into the ground, are all that he needs for the preparation of his material.

The oak sapling is first opened at the broader end by the insertion of a knife blade. Then the other tool is carefully inserted, and forced downwards from butt to tapering end, with the result that three segments peel off outwards. Each of these then has its pith and its bark skimmed away, and the spelk maker is left with three long, pliant wands of sapling oak perhaps two inches or so wide and an inch or less thick. These can then be 'rent' again, until a cluster of wands, a quarter of an inch or even only an eighth of an inch thick remain: tough, pliant, even and eminently suitable for weaving into the basket that will be used by coal merchant, potato grower, fish dealer or textile-mill worker.

The spelk maker, known as a 'spelker' or 'swiller', is still to be found in Lakeland Lancashire, carrying on his country craft as his forefathers did before him. He works as an individual, perhaps in a shed at the foot of his garden, or on his cottage doorstep, or on a low stone wall bordering the village street. He works seated, like the worker in osier, the spelk taking shape between his knees. The bands of oak which he has rent from the sapling are kept permanently moist all the time he is working with them, so that they will be as pliant as possible. They have been soaked, or steamed, in readiness day after day.

Their preparation will have taken him some time, for they are of two types, and must be cunningly matched if the spelk is to be adequate for the job for which it is intended. The oak wands are called either 'spales' or 'taws', 'chissies' or 'tyres', according to whether they are to be used for the uprights or for the interwoven strands, the first being stouter in section than the second.

To prepare the 'spales', the spelker works at a primitive 'horse' similar to that used by the trug maker, using a draw-knife and being very careful as he uses it not to cut across the grain of the oak. Because even greater delicacy of touch is necessary in the preparation of the 'taws', the spelker works the material on his knee, using a thick leather pad to protect his trousers and the flesh beneath them. He sets his knife at a slight angle, and draws the wood towards him, obtaining the right thickness by varying the set of the blade as he does so.

When he has prepared a sufficient number of spales and taws, the spelker prepares to assemble his material and produce his spelk. It consists in the main of the 'bool'—a stout circular, or elliptical, rim that has been steamed and bent round a template just as the trug maker prepares his rims—and of a large number of spales and taws woven criss-cross to make a deep curved bowl. The first stage in the process is to secure what he calls a 'lapping-spale' or two to the 'bool', to give it rigidity. Then, working outwards from each of these, he adds pairs of ribs, or spales, matching them carefully for width and thickness. Each comes to within a fraction of an inch of its neighbour at the point at which it is secured to the 'bool', but the space between them increases as the downward curve of the spelk is developed.

These spaces are filled by the interweaving of the tyres, or chissies, a process corresponding to the osier worker's 'randing'. A spelk made in the old tradition will have what the shipwright calls 'tumble-home'—the inward slope of the ship's side from waterline to deck line and bulwark. The spelk is so designed that it curves outwards for a little way below the 'bool' before beginning its long curve inwards to the centre of the base. This change of curve is obtained by the spelker's drawing his tyres rather more tightly and exerting more pressure on them after the maximum circumference has been passed. He does this, of course, by the feel of the tyres within his fingers, and the finished article will be perfectly symmetrical, whether it is circular or elliptical.

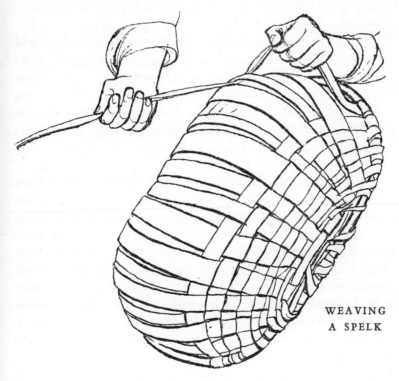

WEAVING
A SPELK

An expert spelker can complete a spelk in three-quarters of an hour or even less, and his product will be an article not only of utility to the man who is going to use it but of beauty; for, like the Sussex trug, it is perfectly designed for the type of job it is to do. The spales and tyres will have dried out by the time the spelk is completed, and will have 'set' in the curve the craftsman's strong fingers have given them. From that time onwards, no matter how heavy, rough or bulky the coal, coke, corn, fish or other commodity carried in it may be, the spelk will retain its attractive, convenient shape: proof of the excellence of an individual craftsman's traditional skill.

Even now the oak's usefulness to the craftsman is not exhausted. Its bark, which previous craftsmen have removed as worthless to them, is of great value in the tanning of raw hide and making it into good leather.

Bark is usually removed from oaks in the spring, for it is only in April, May and early June that this can be done cleanly. First, a ring is cut with an axe round the circumference of the oak at breast height and a second one at ground level. Then, a slit is cut vertically to join the rings. The bark is then beaten all over with a light wooden mallet, which has the effect of loosening it slightly from the sapwood beneath.

Next, the 'barking-iron' is brought into play. This consists of a narrow, sometimes heart-shaped, blade fastened to a short handle. It is inserted into the vertical cut and a steady levering motion applied to it. This eases the bark away from the sapwood, and a skilled craftsman using this simple tool, and his inherited 'know-how', can remove the whole of the bark, even from quite a large tree, in one complete cylinder, broken only at the vertical slit made to take his barking-iron.

Today, this tool is normally made of metal. But in olden times the craftsman used an 'iron' made in fact of the leg-bone of a horse, cut to about a foot in length and sharpened at its smaller end, while the larger end was fitted into a wooden handle in much the same way as primitive tools and weapons were made of bone or flint and wood. Until only the other day there were still some workers in this craft who clung to the barking-iron made of bone in preference to the metal one, just as many people today prefer the old-fashioned shoe-horn to the chromium-plated variety.

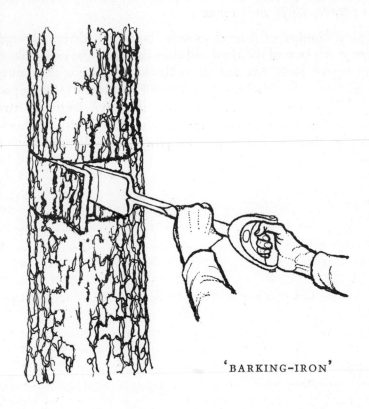

'BARKING-IRON'

Even the sawdust from the oak tree has its use, both for the 'kippering' of herrings and the 'curing' of York hams. The 'galls', those excrescences formed on oak trees by the activities of the gall-fly, have been used from earliest times for the making of ink and certain dyes; and the acorns have long been a favourite with pig breeders, who mix them with the 'mast', or fruit, of the beech tree.

The root, too, has its use for the craftsman. In almost every blacksmith's shop the anvil will be found to be standing on an inverted oak-tree root, deeply embedded in the floor of cement or hard-core or beaten brick and earth, and rigid as if it had been growing there for five hundred years. Its top surfaces and sides have been squared and the anvil itself is secured to the oak block with a number of iron clamps or 'hold-fasts' driven through slots in the base of the anvil and then deep into the end-grain of the timber baulk beneath. It holds the anvil at a convenient height for the blacksmith, and will withstand the impact of sledge-hammer blows as long as the anvil itself: the two materials are bonded to one another and there is little to choose between them for hardness or for powers of endurance. Such is oak.

Craftsmen in Hazel

HAZEL has much in common with osier. Indeed, since both grow very widely, both are very easily 'worked' with the simplest tools, and both can be adapted to a very wide range of use, it is difficult to decide which of the two has proved the greater friend to the country craftsman. There are, in fact, many purposes for which one craftsman will choose hazel and the other osier, and they will be craftsmen each as expert in his craft as the other. On the whole it may be said that hazel is sturdier than osier, being something between a shrub and a tree and growing, as every countryman knows, in coppices.

Country craftsmen discovered the value of hazel so long ago that no one can put a date to the discovery. Wattle fencing, or hazel hurdles, have been used ever since Man began folding sheep on pastureland, particularly when it was open downland—which is one reason why hazel coppices are so plentiful in the south of England, near the downs of Sussex, Berkshire, Hampshire and Wiltshire and the grazing-grounds of East Anglia. Hazel 'spars' have been in use ever since Man began to cover his dwellings with thatch, whether of turf or ling or reed or straw. You cannot go far in the country without taking note of a hundred and one uses for this graceful, thin-skinned, pliant tree, which never grows so big that it cannot be cut down with a bill-hook or a light, single-handed axe.

Hazel cutters, who supply the craftsmen actually working in this light timber, usually buy a complete coppice at so much the acre and fell the poles during the winter, leaving them to lie scattered over the ground until they begin sorting them for their different markets. The smallest and finest are bundled up for sale as pea sticks when pea-planting time comes along; slightly thicker stems and twigs are made up into 'bavins', which are brushwood faggots useful for fire lighting and preferred by the few remaining genuine country bakers of good bread for the firing of their bread ovens. Still larger stems will be made up into bundles to be used as bean sticks later in the year.

With this smaller stuff out of the way, it is possible to sort and grade the genuine hazel 'poles', the largest of which will be of the thickness of a man's wrist and perhaps ten, fifteen or twenty feet long. For these there is an insatiable demand by country craftsmen whose main occupation is to serve the needs of farmers and other agricultural workers.

First and foremost comes the hurdle, whether the three-foot, five-foot or giant six-foot-high variety. Hurdles, or 'wattles', have been in constant use since earliest times. Old engravings show them, hardly differing at all in appearance from those of today, in use well over a thousand years ago, so that they may claim to be among the earliest specimens of Man's handiwork. They are made today exactly as they have always been made, and are likely to continue to be made, for no better method has yet been devised, and there is no really satisfactory substitute for the hazel hurdle.

The craftsman who makes it usually works in the open air within easy reach of the coppice from which he collects his rods, unless he works in a big way, in which case the man who bought the hazel and felled the rods will probably deliver it to his workshop in bulk, trimmed to convenient lengths. Most hurdle makers, however, really prefer to collect and trim their own rods; like the trug makers, they like to have a plentiful supply of prepared material before actually beginning work.

Their equipment could hardly be more simple. The essential is what they refer to as their 'break'. This is a hurdle-making frame consisting of a round or half-round log rather more than

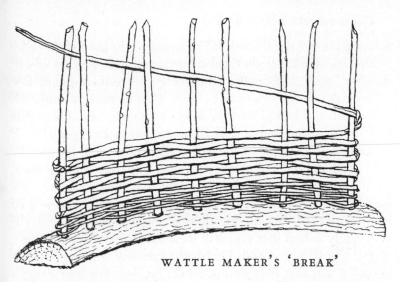

WATTLE MAKER'S 'BREAK'

six feet in length and lying on its side sunk a few inches into the
ground to give it steadiness. In this log the hurdle maker has
drilled eight or nine holes, about an inch in diameter and about
eight or nine inches apart, in a straight line along the upper surface. This is his 'bench'. It sets the proportions of every hurdle he
will make, and will last him half a lifetime or more.

For the standard hurdle he uses three types of hazel. The
stoutest rods, approximately an inch thick and three, four, five,
or six feet long according to the height of the hurdle he is to make,
are first stood upright in the 'break', the two at the extreme ends
being the thickest. These uprights are known to him as 'sails'.
The second type of rod, rather smaller than the 'sails', is cleft
down the centre and used for the main body of the hurdle. The
third type of hazel is a much thinner rod, used 'in the round', and
woven only into the top and the bottom 'courses' of the hurdle.
He refers to these as his 'ethers', and their interweaving among the
sails is a process known as 'ethering'.

Having set his eight or nine sails in his break, the hurdle maker
first takes a number of these finger-thin ethers, to which he has
given a fine tapering point with a shrewd stroke of his curved
knife blade. He begins to work a few uprights from the end one,

61

weaving his ethers outwards till he comes to the last rod. In order to bind his hurdle together, these horizontal rods, first the ethers, then the 'splits', and finally, when he comes to the topmost few inches, half a dozen or so more ethers, must be passed round each outside sail and locked into the lower courses in such a way that they do not spring out and so allow the hurdle to expand.

Here is an example of the true craftsman's secret. If you take hold of a hazel rod and proceed to bend it sharply back on itself, the chances are a hundred to one that it will snap; at the very least its skin and outer fibres will tear away, and the rod will be badly weakened. But the hurdle maker can avoid this, and it is very rarely indeed that you will see a hurdle in which there is a snapped, or damaged, rod. He has the knack of bending his rods in such a way that they do not break. He does this by putting a twist into the rod at the same time as he bends it back, so that the bend is a sort of spiral and the strain on the fibres is equalized among them. Have a look at a hazel rod bent in this way—and then try to do it for yourself!

He works, of course, from the bottom upwards. A few rows of ethers, the pointed end of the last one slanted diagonally down-wards and locked into the tight grip of the first two rows. Then follow row upon row of stouter, split hazel, rising to within a few inches of the top of the hurdle, hammered well down so that they fit closely together and run horizontally, leaving only a thin gap here and there for the wind to blow through. And finally, the top few rows of ethers, with the last pair slanted off down-wards to lock the whole into position. No amount of swelling from the damp, or rough handling by the shepherd, will loosen these top ethers. The final twist he has given them produces a vice-like grip on the end sails, and though the hurdle, even if it is six feet high, is a lightweight, it will take a tremendous amount of punishment during its long life.

When the hurdle is complete, it is lifted out of the break and the lower ends of the sails are roughly pointed so that the hurdle can if necessary be driven into the turf and stand upright without other support. Usually, of course, they are fastened together to form rectangles, supporting one another in this way, or are braced against stout posts driven into the ground. But in themselves they are very rigid indeed. Especially those which have been woven on a break which has been given a very slight curve. This is done deliberately, so that when the hurdle is removed the natural springiness in the hazels forces it out straight again and compresses the 'weave'.

There are certain features in a hurdle demanded by certain types of user. For example, anyone who has ever had to carry a six-foot-high hurdle, particularly in a wind, will know how difficult it is to carry and control. Shepherds on windswept downland may have to spend much of their time lifting and replacing hurdles as they move their flocks over the pasture. The craftsman therefore inserts into the hurdles a pair of conveniently placed hand-holds, known as 'twillies', to enable the shepherd to move them about more easily.

A rather specialized type of hurdle made by the same craftsman is a circular one. It is constructed on a break resembling a very large wheel partly embedded in the ground and drilled with holes some eight or nine inches apart as for the standard type of hurdle. In the lower part of the hurdle, however, gaps are left through which individual sheep can poke their heads and eat hay brought to the spot when for some reason or other the grazing is insufficient for them. This is just one of many examples which could be quoted to illustrate how the country craftsman turns his special skill to the service of the men who depend on agriculture for their livelihood; as, of course, he does himself, indirectly.

The hurdle maker is also very often the maker of 'spars', though these are needed in such enormous quantities for thatching that there are also many craftsmen working in hazel who give the whole of their time to this particular activity.

Spars—also known in various parts of the country as 'spics', 'tangs', 'sparrods', 'roovers', 'brotches', 'splints', 'scollops' and 'withynecks'—are the hazel pegs used by the thatcher to pin down the upper layer of thatch on to its foundation, which may be old thatch, or heather, or brushwood or some other suitable material.

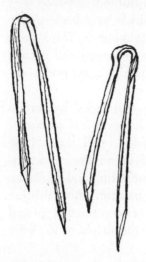

To look at, a spar resembles an out-size hairpin with 'legs' anything up to twenty-four inches long and more, though one of these is ordinarily a little shorter than the other.

It may look simple to make; and indeed, to the spar maker it is simple enough. The essence of making it is to bend it double in such a way that not only is the hazel rod not broken, or its fibres cracked and split, but it retains most of its original springiness. The spar maker selects rods that are straight and not more than two inches thick at the most. With his bill-hook he cuts them to length and also splits each rod down the centre. Rods of this size split easily. There is no need for him to use anything more elaborate by way of tool than his trusty bill-hook, but he will probably have a stout pole driven into the ground close beside him, and when he has opened the butt-end of each rod, will force it against the pole in such a way that, with a little gentle leverage, the hazel splits evenly from end to end, leaving the grain unbroken, or, as he terms it, not letting the grain 'run out'.

THATCHER'S 'SPARS'

The half-rounds are then cleft a second time in the same way, so that each two-inch rod produces four quarter-rods, each having two flat, white sides and one rounded side with the bark still on it. A sharp cut or two with his bill-hook, and he has put a square-cut point on each end of the spar; then, using the same technique as the hurdle maker uses for the ethers and other hazels to bind the hurdle together, a swift double twist, the craftsman bends each quarter-rod in two, with one leg slightly shorter than the other, and the spar is made.

Spars, however, must be supplied in enormous quantities, and this means bundling them for transport to the site where the thatcher is about to begin his work. Bundling springy hazel is not as easy as one might suppose, but the hazel worker has devised a gadget for this purpose which is as simple as anything could be, and so efficient that no better device has come along to take its place, even in this age of invention. It is known as a 'woodman's grip', and every country craftsman whose work entails bundling hazel or other springy wood has one beside him for just this purpose.

It consists of two fairly stout stakes perhaps three or four feet long and linked together part way along their length by a piece of strong cord or twine, a turn or two of which is taken round the loose rods that are to be bundled together. With the lower ends of the stakes pressed on to the ground, the woodman forces the

WOODMAN'S 'GRIP'

upper ends outwards by gripping each and straightening his arms. The leverage of course can be varied according to the position on the stakes in which the cord is tied.

When the bundle has been sufficiently constricted he braces his knees against the stakes, bends down and rapidly passes a noose of twine, or a withy, round it, one at each end. Then he straightens up, the stakes fall to the ground, and the bundle, faggot or 'bavin' lies securely bound at his feet. It is simple as that; completely fool-proof; and it works every time!

A more highly specialized use for hazel than either hurdle or spar has been found by the salmon trappers, particularly those working on the salmon reaches of the Wye and Severn. They are not rod-and-line anglers, of course, but genuine trappers—and unpopular, therefore, with the sporting angler because of what is held to be the unsporting nature of catching this much-prized fish.

The salmon trapper uses a 'putcher', which he makes for him-self on the lines of the putchers that have been in use there for generations back, possibly even for centuries, made of hazel from the handy Forest of Dean. He cuts his rods in the autumn and allows them to season throughout the winter before beginning to work on them in the spring. He will probably have as many as three or four dozen of these putchers by the time the season opens, and when salmon trapping is in full swing there may be several thousand of them altogether in the wide estuaries and desolate mud flats.

Like almost all the products of craftsmen working in natural materials, the putcher is an object not only of utility but of beauty. It is, in essence, a basket; but a basket-with-a-difference. In fact, it is an open basketwork cone five or six feet long and two feet wide at its larger end, tapering almost to a point. Its making calls for highly specialized knowledge and manual skill, and the number of putcher makers becomes smaller with every passing year.

As usual, however, the equipment necessary for constructing

it is simple in the extreme. The craftsman works on a 'break' differing from
most in the fact that it can be rotated.
This saves him the trouble of moving
about during the long and elaborate
process of making the putcher. It consists simply of two discs, one about two
feet in diameter and the other very
small. Both are mounted on a pole
driven into the ground, and can be
rotated round it by a touch of the hand.
Each disc contains a dozen or so holes,
the ones in the larger disc tallying exactly
with the number in the smaller disc, but
being of course much wider apart.

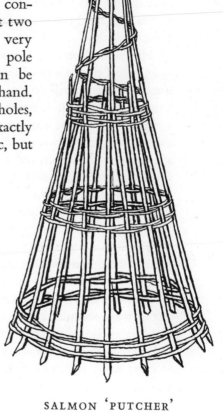

SALMON 'PUTCHER'

PUTCHER MAKER'S 'BREAK'

The putcher maker likes if possible to work on a high stool or upturned barrel or, failing all else, a tree stump. He starts off by inserting a number of hazel rods in the holes of the lower disc and the corresponding holes of the upper disc, some craftsmen preferring the larger disc to be at the bottom, others the smaller disc. In any case they are about five feet apart. The result of this first stage is that he has what looks like a very long, tapering, open-sided bird-cage.

He then selects some much thinner hazel rods, of about the diameter of the 'ethers' of the hurdle maker, or even a bundle of osiers, for either will do provided the main framework is of the stronger hazel rods. A few rows of these thinner rods are interwoven through the main framework a little below the upper disc and above the lower disc. Then, at further intervals, he inserts a few more thin rods, using them 'in the round', not cleft. So quick-fingered is he that he can join thin rod to thin rod and interweave a continuous spiral so that no join is apparent unless you look very closely indeed. He calls this long, thin spiral the 'worm', and it is a very appropriate name for it.

The finished putcher consists of three joined sections, known to him as the 'mouthpiece', the 'diddle' and the 'wheel'. It will be nearly six feet long in all, tapering from twenty-four inches to only a couple of inches or so. The 'girdles' of thin hazel mark out its three sections. Because of the stout hazel rods that constitute the main framework and the thinner interwoven rods, it will be very strong; but it will also be so light that he will be able to carry half a dozen of them or more slung about his shoulders, when he leaves his garden workshop and sets off for the river bank. Outwardly the putcher will be smooth and innocent looking, but it contains one or two spikes, cunningly inserted into a strategic position so that the salmon, having once entered it, cannot turn round and escape.

Putchers are erected in 'batteries' three or four deep and mounted on a sturdy framework of timbers driven deep into the river bed that may stretch for some hundreds of yards across the

mud flats where experience has shown that salmon are likely to
run when the tide covers them. It is largely the tide on which the
trapper relies to bring the salmon into his putcher and force it
from the easy open end well down into the 'nose' where it will
be firmly held by the weight of water flowing in behind it. This
trap is so fixed on the trestles which carry it that the weight of the
salmon in the nose of it will cause it to tilt downwards slightly.
Like many other fish, the salmon can be 'drowned' if it is held
motionless for too long in this way. The salmon trapper knows
this. Having set his putchers at low tide, either with the open end
downstream in order to catch the incoming salmon, or with the
open end upstream, to catch the salmon travelling on the ebb-
tide, he can return to his cottage and do a bit of gardening, or
follow his regular employment, until the time comes to go and
inspect his putchers at next low tide and claim his booty. A
putcher is very simple, and very efficient indeed.

The craft of putcher making is not by any means the only one
to be found along the river banks of Wye and Severn and other
rivers of the Welsh Border. Older, in all probability, by many
hundreds of years is the craft of coracle making, which was
certainly practised more than two thousand years ago. Today
only a bare handful of men, mainly Welshmen and Border
dwellers, ply this ancient craft; but it is a craft with an unbroken
tradition older than most that we have so far considered.

After the primitive and clumsy dug-out, the coracle is the
oldest type of boat known in Britain. It consists of nothing more
than a framework of hazel, sometimes mixed with osier, and a
'skin' of tarred canvas stretched over it—the 'modern' successor
to the animal hide used by the present-day coracle maker's
remote ancestors. It is not peculiar to such rivers as Wye and
Severn, Towy, Teifi and Dee but is to be seen also on the Boyne,
in Ireland, and the Spey in Scotland, and also on the waters round
the Hebrides. It is, of course, a one-man boat. It rarely exceeds
five or six feet in length, the length of a putcher, and is rarely
more than twelve inches deep. It has no keel, and is therefore

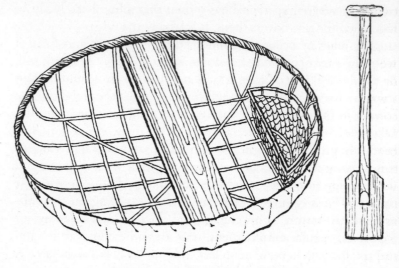

THE CORACLE AND PADDLE

unsuitable for use in open water, though the men who paddle in them show an astonishing degree of watermanship in remaining safely afloat when strong winds spring up and lash the rivers into waves.

The craftsman who makes the coracle is usually the owner too. He uses selected hazel for the main part of the framework, though he does not object to using good osiers to 'fill in', and sometimes, if ash is plentiful in his neighbourhood, will cleave thin slats of ash and add these too. Whatever wood he uses, he is careful to see that none of the grain has been cut through during the process of preparation with axe, fromard or knife.

Very often the actual rim of his coracle is made of thin hazel rods twisted almost like rope, to give it resilience greater than it would have if the rim were a single bent rod, even if its over-all thickness were greater. The twisting and intertwining of the pliant hazel make it possible for the framework to withstand the stretching that is caused by the weight of the occupant, and also the pressure caused by the water in which it floats. In fact, the two opposed 'pressures' will help the twisted hazels to compact together and gain in strength.

The 'hull' of the coracle is constructed by plaiting and inter-weaving great numbers of thin, wide, pliant strips of cleft hazel, or osier or other similar wood, criss-cross and spiral-wise, in such a way as to give it shape and a fair degree of rigidity and resilience combined. But the coracle maker must bear in mind certain other necessities, in exactly the same way as the hurdle maker had to bear in mind the requirements of the shepherd who had to man-handle his hurdles. A light seat is incorporated into the frame-work while it is still being woven—the position for the seat having to be very carefully calculated with the occupant's weight in mind. A creel to take the fisherman's catch is also very often incorporated into the interior of the hull; possibly one at each end to enable the fisherman to balance his craft. For it weighs so little, and is so smoothly rounded beneath him, that it is necessary to 'sit' the coracle with the utmost accuracy.

When the framework is completed, the canvas, or even calico, is stretched over it, fastened firmly to it at the rim, and given several coats of good, thick tar to make it absolutely watertight. The craft really is no more than a basket, without stem-post, stern-post, keel or rudder. Its over-all length will be hardly six feet; its 'beam' will be something between four and five feet; its 'draught' only a matter of inches. A man who is to occupy and paddle such a vessel needs to be just about as much of a craftsman as the man who constructed it—and indeed it is often the same person who does both. A touch of the paddle too strongly on one side or the other, and the near-circular boat will start spinning on the water like a tee to tum until the occupant is too dizzy to care whether it sinks or not!

Even a full-size one weighs little more than ten or twelve pounds at most. Its owner may live some distance from the water where he goes fishing, but he will keep his coracle up-ended or upside down, and out of the sun, in his garden, and when he wants to use it, will slip it over his head and walk to the river bank looking like a giant black snail-shell with a pair of short legs poking out beneath it, or a black beetle walking on its hind legs!

Hazel combines great strength—particularly 'tensile' strength —with pliancy. It is for this reason much in demand for the making of hoops to bind the lightweight staves of the cheaper type of barrels made to contain what are called 'dry goods', such as cheese, sugar and so on. Such barrels are generally known as 'slack casks' and you will often see them in grocers' and green-grocers' shops, containing nuts or new potatoes or cheap grapes in sawdust. They do not need to be very strong, still less to be watertight; hazel hoops, therefore, are highly suitable because they are strong enough, and very much cheaper than iron hoops would be.

Hoop makers, still to be found in Sussex, in some parts of the Midlands and in the Furness district of Lancashire, work with very simple tools: a 'break' something like the trug maker's 'horse'; a sharp knife; possibly a fromard, and a draw-knife; and an axe or bill-hook if the craftsman has to cut his hazels himself.

He selects the best hazel he can find, cleaves it in the same way as the hurdle and spar makers and others do, being extremely careful not to split the grain at any point, and then proceeds to fine-down the flat, white surface with his draw-knife until he has produced a thin, even band, pliant and strong. He usually leaves the skin on the outer, curved surface, which contrasts nicely with the white wood of which the staves have been made.

If his hazel rods are still green, they are easy to bend into perfect circles, measured to fit the various types of 'slack cask' for which they are intended. He works to a prepared hoop, cut to length, bent to a perfect circle and nailed securely so that it will not spring. If, as is more usual, he has to work with dry, or seasoned, hazel, then he must either soak or steam it before working on it. Some of his rods, designed to make hoops for the largest slack casks, may be twelve or fourteen feet in length and will make hoops four feet and more in diameter even with the nailed overlap.

There are various methods of 'rounding' a length of hazel rod so that it grows naturally into a near circle and then needs only the minimum of shaping before it is nailed. One of these is to draw each length through a specially constructed 'break'—the word is used by the country craftsman for a wide variety of such things. It will consist of a stout beam with a well-rounded wooden bar, or small log, fixed to it and also a movable bar of metal or some hardwood. The lengths of hazel will be drawn across the rounded bar while with the other bar the craftsman exerts the pressure by leverage, so that the hazel is forced to assume a regular curve throughout its passage. In much the same way iron workers will shape a piece of cold iron or mild steel. After being pulled between these two 'jaws', the length of hazel will come to assume the right natural curve, and the two ends can then be overlapped and securely nailed to one another.

Another, and much more elaborate, type of break is used by hoop makers who have to make a wide range of hoops, from very small and light to large and com-paratively heavy. It consists of a stout pole driven firmly into the ground, or the workshop floor. From it there stick out radially a set of eight 'spokes' of hardwood, each rigidly attached to the cen-tral pole level with all the others. Into each of these eight spokes a number of hardwood pegs are inserted, pointing upwards, every one of them spaced at regular intervals along the spoke to tally exactly with those on the other spokes.

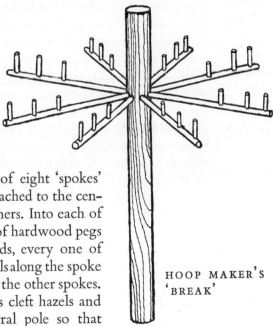

HOOP MAKER'S
'BREAK'

The hoop maker takes his cleft hazels and winds them round the central pole so that they press strongly outwards against the

73

appropriate pegs on the eight spokes. Because the pegs are equidistant from the centre, the result is that the hazel automatically takes on a perfectly circular form. When each one is shaped, the hoop maker grips the overlapping ends in a pair of pliers, removes the hoop and nails the ends together. This may sound a complicated and laborious process, but in fact it is very rapid indeed. The natural springiness in the hazel forces it outwards against the peg and the only shape it can assume is that of a circle. A good hoop maker will quickly pile up a score or more of hoops, every one of them the same as every other to within a fraction of an inch.

There are a very great number of uses for hazel which are not particularly the concern of the individual craftsman, and before we look at what is perhaps the strangest of all hazel crafts we may just mention these briefly: some of them you may already have noticed for yourselves; others you will notice if you keep a keen look out in the right parts of the country.

Because hazel stands up well to the action of water, it was used by prehistoric 'Lake Dwellers' in regions like Glastonbury. These communities built groups of wattle huts on foundations consisting of great faggots of hazels laid in shallow water. This enabled them to live in comparative security from wild animals and marauding and predatory tribes. Archaeologists excavating in such districts have found these faggots still in fairly good order, though they tend to disintegrate when they are exposed to the fresh air.

Using this knowledge, railway engineers like George Stephenson, and others after him, laid foundations of hazel faggots for furlongs at a stretch across boggy ground; road engineers made use of hazel faggots both for drainage purposes and for reinforcing embankments, especially where the soil was what they call 'friable' and so needed binding together. This use of hazel for reinforcing sand or mud is seen at its most spectacular in Holland, where the gigantic land-reclaiming schemes in the IJsselmeer are still in progress. Bundles, or 'pads', of hazel many yards wide and long and several feet thick are woven together and laid at a slope, pegged down with enormous spars, to hold the soil in position until the stonework of the causeways and breakwaters has been completed. The hazel is not only water-resistant, it is astonishingly tough; you will often see ships' fenders consisting of big faggots of hazel lashed together and slung over the side to take the pressure of the ship against the quayside as the tide rises and falls.

But certainly the strangest use of hazel is that made by the craftsman who goes by the curious name of 'dowser', or water diviner. Though other materials are used by these dowsers, including springy metal, the great majority of them prefer hazel to anything else: they are practising a very ancient craft—one that goes back into the mists of time and was known in many parts of the world—and, like all men who work according to an old tradition, keep to their traditional methods.

There are people who do not believe in water divining at all, and talk casually of 'just luck', 'pure chance', and so on. But people who live in remote country districts, where 'mains water' is still no more than a dream, and particularly in districts where there is limestone and chalk beneath the soil, never doubt the water diviner's expertise. Farmers who need large and unfailing quantities for watering their stock, and other country dwellers who need it in lesser but still regular quantities—the cottage folk and so on—are absolutely dependent on this very individual craftsman whose craft, even compared with others we have seen demanding a high degree of inherited skill and 'know-how', smacks rather of magic than of anything more ordinary.

In times of drought, springs tend to dry up and wells to lose their level of water; even in normal summers, where there is limestone, as in the high Pennines, or chalk, as along the South Downs, there is always the risk of water shortage. Underground channels that may have had water flowing through them since as far back as people in the district can remember sometimes unaccountably dry up. It is in circumstances like these that the dowser comes into his own.

He is sometimes a specialist, widely known in the region and operating almost full-time; sometimes he is a farm labourer, a shopkeeper, a postman, a policeman or indeed anyone living in the country. His name and address will be known, however, to people for many miles around; in his way he is hardly less important than the doctor or the district nurse.

His equipment must surely be the simplest of any craftsman's equipment in any branch of craft: all he requires is a hazel twig! He will cut it for himself from the handiest hazel coppice, selecting a stem no thicker than a pencil, forked symmetrically into two smaller stems of equal thickness. He cuts off the stem an inch or two below the fork, and trims the two thinner stems to about eight or nine inches in length. This gives him a 'Y'-shaped hazel 'twig' not unlike one that you may cut to make a catapult, only of course thinner by a great deal and with the butt much shorter and the arms much longer.

The water diviner, or dowser, invariably works alone. He prefers to have no one within hailing distance of him. If you ever have the good luck to see one at work you will notice that even children, who seem to have a knack of turning up wherever anything unusual or interesting is going on, are absent from the scene. The locating of water at a time of shortage is far too important a matter for country folk to risk upsetting the dowser by allowing their children to follow him about!

The manner in which he holds his hazel 'divining rod' is peculiar and all-important. He walks with his elbows held in close to his sides and the lower part of his arms extended horizontally in front of him, the palms of his hands turned uppermost. The edges of his hands will be practically touching. With his fingers curled down towards his palms and his thumbs extended outwards, he grips the two springy ends of his 'Y'-shaped rod in such a way that its short butt is pointing forwards and a little upwards at the same time. The rod will therefore be in a permanent state of tension—which is the whole secret of success. The grip between the thumb and the first finger of each hand must remain

DOWSER'S HAZEL TWIG AND GRIP

constant and firm, so that it is impossible for the two ends of the rod to turn in the slightest.

The dowser begins to 'quarter' the field or yard or whatever piece of ground it may be beneath which the owner hopes to find that there is hidden water. The nearer it is to his farm, or cottage, of course, the better pleased he will be, for this will save him time and labour in fetching and carrying water, or the cost of piping if he is intending to have it laid on to his premises. He walks perhaps twenty, thirty, fifty or a hundred paces forward in one direction; then a similar distance at right angles to his first, and all the time he is keenly aware of the slender divining rod that is held in tension between his outstretched hands. He is waiting for the first tiny suggestion of movement that will tell him that he is 'getting warm'.

His aim, of course, is to criss-cross the ground, narrowing and narrowing the area of his search for water, until finally he is able to pin-point it exactly. In a way, what he is doing is similar to the old-fashioned game that children sometimes play, when as they approach nearer and nearer to the hidden object someone keeps on telling them they are getting 'warmer', or 'colder'; but in his case, of course, the information is given by his hazel rod.

The first intimation the dowser receives that he is nearing some hidden underground stream or reservoir is when, in spite of his firm and unyielding grip on the springy arms of his rod, the short butt-end begins to twist, either upwards or downwards. The movement may be so slight that no one but a keen-eyed dowser himself would be able to detect it. In fact, he feels the movement, rather than sees it; he is made conscious of it by that inner sense which almost all craftsmen possess in greater or lesser degree. To him it is the vital clue.

Having become conscious that the hazel is stirring, that the short end is moving ever so slightly upwards or downwards in spite of his grip on the two arms of the rod, he checks his pacing and works backwards, watching for the point at which the rod reverts to its original position. And there he plants a small wooden peg in the turf, and turns a right angle, to continue his pacing to and fro in order to locate the point at which the movement of his rod will be most pronounced.

He may discover this almost at once; on the other hand he may have to continue his search for quite a long time afterwards, in order to find the point at which the quantity, or 'flow', of the underground water is strongest. Half a pocketful of pegs—hazel pegs, in all probability, cleft with a shrewd cut of his knife blade so that they have a white surface to catch the eye when he has stuck them in the ground—may have been used before he finishes. He may have been several hours on the job. If he has, it will be seen that there is sweat on his brow, and his hands, the strong hands of a countryman, have a tendency to tremble, for to control the movement of a piece of thin, springy hazel, which any child could twist and break with ease, in such a way that it tells a complete story of underground water demands a tremendous degree of concentration.

The dowser is able to interpret the movements of his divining rod. He knows by the strength of the movement of the butt just how near, or far away, the hidden water lies; he knows by its upward or downward movement in which direction it is running, and the strength of its flow. He does not merely guess; from long experience he *knows*. The majority of dowsers work on the basis 'no water, no payment'; and it is very rare indeed for a dowser to have to confess himself wrong in his 'diagnosis'.

He will be generously paid, for water is essential to everyone. But, being the good craftsman he is, it is likely that he will derive hardly less satisfaction from seeing the well diggers or bore-hole sinkers at work where he left his final peg, and the water springing up to the surface, clear and cool and plentiful, than he will from the money that jingles in his pocket when he has received his payment for a job completed. He may return on the day when the other workers depart, and dip a glass into the water that he has 'divined', while the owner of the land does the same, toasting one another in the oldest and most invaluable of all known drinks. And as he goes on his way, he may keep an eye cocked when he comes to a hazel coppice, and snip off a nice rod, to be trimmed in readiness for the next time he is sent for to practise this ancient and essential craft.

Craftsmen in Beech

Unlike the oak tree, which goes on growing for five hundred years, maturing all the time, and lives on to a very ripe and sturdy old age, the beech tree rarely lives for more than two hundred years and is fully 'grown up' by the time it has reached its first century. It is a noble tree, characterized by a very smooth bark from the lowest point of its great trunk right through its enormous lower boughs, its upper branches and its lesser branches that produce the deepest shade to be found anywhere in our forests, except perhaps among very close-set conifers.

You will see it at its finest where there is chalk or limestone beneath the soil, which is one reason why there is so much splendid beech on the Berkshire and Sussex Downs, on the Cotswolds, and—most notably of all, perhaps—on the lovely Chiltern Hills. But it is a far traveller, too: if you have been into Perthshire you will probably have seen the famous beech 'hedge' of Meikleour—a solid quarter-mile of ninety-foot-high beeches, six hundred and more of them.

Like oak, beech has weight and great strength. Unlike oak, however, it does not stand up well to the effects of weather; for this reason it is a timber for use indoors rather than outdoors. Craftsmen down the ages have found a myriad uses for it. Fortunately it propagates itself very well; but even so, the Forestry Commission recently planted six million young beech trees, being well aware that the demand for it among craftsmen is always greater than the supply.

The great merit of this fine timber is that, though it is very hard, and in the right conditions immensely durable, its grain is so close, and of such quality, that the craftsman can work beech not only the way of the grain—as he does with oak and other strongly grained timbers—but across the grain; in fact, in any direction whatsoever. Not only has it this most useful quality, but it is less likely than almost any other timber to warp under changes of temperature or sheer strain. It is therefore always in great demand by men making objects, large or small, in which accuracy and permanence of shape and proportion are of prime importance.

An excellent example of the use of beech for this sort of purpose is seen in the making of pianos—a craftsman's job if ever there was one! The stresses set up by the stringing of a piano, particularly those of the heavy wires for the bass clef of a grand piano, are enormous. For this reason, the so-called 'wrest-planks', those elaborately jointed and angled main spars in a piano frame, are very often made of beech. So important is it that there shall be no suspicion of warping or shrinkage during the whole lifetime of the instrument that the beech used for the frame is sawn, as the craftsman says, 'on the quarter', which adds an extra guarantee of rigidity to the timber he is to shape. And because beech has such a close, fine grain, he can fashion it most delicately, so that the frame is an object of beauty as well as of great strength.

Beech is the choice of furniture makers, particularly for the frames of large pieces such as deeply sprung and heavily upholstered armchairs and sofas, on which the weight of heavy persons may be unevenly and carelessly distributed as they lounge at their ease. It is the choice, too, of coach builders who want rigidity and permanence in parts of their construction work and do not mind the weight that beech possesses. You will find a good deal of beech in the frames of station-waggons, for instance.

Because beech generally is more serviceable indoors than out, it has always been the choice of craftsmen making things for the home. One of the oldest crafts that still survive—though it looks as if its days now are numbered—in furniture making is that of the chair 'bodger', whose base has always been and still remains the beechwoods of the Chilterns. It is because these particular beechwoods have flourished so abundantly, and for so long, that small country towns like High Wycombe are still, today, centres of the furniture-making industry. The chair bodger remains a humble, individual craftsman, but he plays an important part, even in this highly mechanized age, in the making of furniture.

Like the hazel hurdle maker, his 'workshop' is the place where he finds his material. Until only a very few years ago the beechwoods on the Chilterns seemed to be filled with these modest workshops—little more than brushwood-covered huts in which a craftsman, or perhaps a couple of craftsmen, worked quietly with the simplest of equipment, in the tradition of their forefathers. Today you may have difficulty in locating more than an odd one here and there; tomorrow, perhaps the last of them will have laid down his tools and retired from a lifetime of chair bodging, while their sons will have taken up some mechanical employment in a factory dominated by automation.

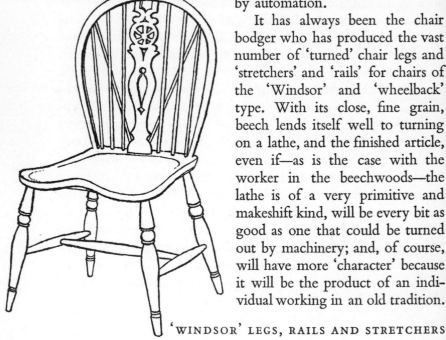

It has always been the chair bodger who has produced the vast number of 'turned' chair legs and 'stretchers' and 'rails' for chairs of the 'Windsor' and 'wheelback' type. With its close, fine grain, beech lends itself well to turning on a lathe, and the finished article, even if—as is the case with the worker in the beechwoods—the lathe is of a very primitive and makeshift kind, will be every bit as good as one that could be turned out by machinery; and, of course, will have more 'character' because it will be the product of an individual working in an old tradition.

'WINDSOR' LEGS, RAILS AND STRETCHERS

CHAIR BODGER'S 'POLE LATHE'

And it will indeed be an old tradition. There are old engravings showing 'lathes' in use centuries ago which hardly differ in the slightest from those made and used by the Chiltern chair bodgers today. Like so many pieces of equipment evolved by the craftsman for his own use, it is extremely simple in design, simple in operation, and effective for the job it has been devised to perform.

The chair bodger works as near to his raw material as he can. Beneath the canopy of close-set beech leaves, which offer protection from the weather, though he will probably erect a workshop for himself of four beech poles, a few branches laid across them and some brushwood on top of those, he will establish himself. His 'bench' will be a stump of beech cut to a convenient height to work at. On this he will do his rougher work—the cleaving of segments of beech and the chopping up of 'waste' for humbler purposes than chair-leg making.

The main piece of equipment, however, is his 'pole lathe'. This consists of a solid framework, firmly embedded in the ground, from which a pair of 'poppet-heads' stand up; one of them fixed, the other capable of being adjusted for position by being slid along between the two main timbers. These correspond to the 'chuck' of the engineer's lathe. Between them, the roughly shaped beech that is to be turned into a leg, rail or stretcher is placed horizontally.

Just in front of the lathe bed, a stump of beech is driven into the ground and to it a long, tapering, 'whippy' piece of beech is secured in such a way that its point is immediately over the lathe bed at a height of a yard or so. From it there hangs a piece of twine. The twine is wound a couple of times round the piece of beech that is to be turned, and the free end then attached to a simple treadle which the chair bodger operates by alternately pressing his foot on it and releasing it. And that is the whole of his lathe!

The first process, of course, is to prepare the beech roughly for the actual turning. He works at it while it is still 'green', the process of seasoning taking place after the leg or rail or stretcher has been turned. He uses a cross-cut saw to cut his timber to length, after which it is laid aside and he turns to the usual tools of the timber worker: the axe, mallet and froe, and the draw-knife.

According to the size of the beech bole on which he is working he uses axe or froe to produce first a semi-circular piece and then a quarter-segment. These are further cleft until he has a number of triangular pieces, each of them slightly larger than the finished product is to be. The thin edge that has been the very heart of the beech is trimmed away with the froe, and the other two corners equally, until he has a roughly five-sided bar of wood, not one of square section. This is because he would have difficulty in turning a square into a round section, whereas with the five-sided piece his simple tools will be perfectly effective, once he has trimmed them a little with his draw-knife. He uses this also to do the preliminary tapering-off of each wooden bar, so as to save time when he comes to use his lathe.

Then, he centres his piece of timber between the two poppet-heads of his pole lathe, picks up the first of his chisels, plucks deftly at the twine after he has taken a turn or two round the wood, and at the same moment presses down on his treadle. The wood spins in the lathe and he makes the first cut in it, releasing his chisel from the wood and at the same time his foot from the treadle so that the springiness of the pole overhead can pull the twine upwards and, as it were, 'unroll' the wood in readiness for the next cut. This is, in fact, the only basic difference between the pole lathe of the chair bodger and the engineer's lathe: he can cut only on the downward movement of the treadle; he must then momentarily hold his chisel clear while the wood spins back again. It might be thought that this would mean a great deal of wasted time, but in fact the chair bodger, from long practice, works with great speed, the wood spinning between the poppet-heads and the beech bough rising and falling with a steady, springy motion that is full of rhythm.

There is a tradition about the various rings cut into the legs, and the proportions of curve and taper, which the chair bodger adheres to very closely. He works by eye and feel, of course, like all other craftsmen, but you might lay a hundred legs side by side, and would find it difficult to spot any two of them that varied by more than a hair's breadth—just enough, let us say, to make the difference between the hand-made and the machine-made product.

These chair legs, rails and stretchers are turned out by the thousand, even by the hundred thousand, in this manner. They are then stacked, criss-cross so that the fresh air can pass between them, for seasoning in the open before being collected and delivered to the chair makers in High Wycombe and elsewhere. Stacked on the ground among the great beech trees which still remain to be felled, they look curiously slight and insubstantial. The fact is, however, that because the timber of which they were made was cleft, not sawn down lengthwise, they are very strong indeed. Draw-knife and lathe between them may have whittled away a great deal of wood, but they are strong enough for a lifetime of service, and there are many Windsor and similar chairs in use on rough kitchen floors in farmhouses and cottages up and down the country which have served three and four generations and more of the same family and are as strong and rigid today as they were when the craftsmen made them.

Beech is very largely knot-free, which is a great advantage when it is being worked by the humble chair bodger or by the craftsman in a piano factory or furniture-making workshop. It has not such a long record of service as hazel, for example; but because of the closeness and fineness of its grain, combined with its hardness, the craftsman turned more and more to it as his skill in manipulating timber increased and his armoury of tools for working it developed. He quickly found, for example, what good tool handles could be made of beech: it could be readily shaped to his hand, it was firm to grasp, it did not warp or shrink, and it looked well, too. He did not use it for the handles of heavy tools and implements like axes, sledge-hammers, picks, and so on, since these were much used out of doors and he really wanted something lighter in weight and with rather more 'whip' in it than beech possesses. But for small tools it was ideal.

The carpenter found it exactly right for his growing armoury of chisels and gouges, the handles of his screwdrivers, saws, gimlets and bradawls. It was smooth, easily turned, and hard enough to stand up to the blows of his mallet without splitting or 'shaking'. It would grip the tapering spindle of his chisel relentlessly, even after years of heavy use. Today, though there are many craftsmen who prefer the smooth, hard, yellow box wood for the handles of such tools, in spite of the extra cost, there are even greater numbers who stick to beech for their handles as their fathers and forefathers before them did. If you look at the array of beech-handled chisels and gouges set in slots behind or above a joiner's bench you may think that all the handles are identical. But the joiner himself, who is using them all, and every day, will know instantly, by the feel of it, which tool he has picked up. The hard beech handle will, with years of use, have taken to itself some microscopic differences of surface and texture which will communicate themselves to the horny palm of the man who uses the tool.

Except where metal is used, beech is invariably the choice of material for the carpenter's and joiner's planes, whether they are the small and beautifully fashioned 'smoothing' plane or the big jack plane or 'shooting' plane. It is essential to him that the body of his plane shall be absolutely square and free from the slightest tendency to warp or shrink, and it must retain these properties throughout its long and strenuous life.

A beechwood plane, if you examine it closely, is a beautiful example of craftsmanship in itself—made by a craftsman for a craftsman. The narrow slot is cut accurately into the 'sole' of the plane, the wedge-shaped 'escapement' rising in the body of the plane above this slot has a subtle slant to it nicely calculated by the maker to take the blade, or 'cutter', and the 'back iron' which gives it strength and rigidity, and to hold them at exactly the right angle to the run of the plane to produce work of the right standard. The handle of a plane (other than the short smoothing planes which have no handles at all but are contained within the joiner's hands) is a beautifully curved and calculated piece of carved beechwood to which the palm, fingers and thumb fit as though designed for it, instead of the handle being designed for them.

Beech is ideal, too, for the square, wedge-shaped carpenter's mallet. A head made of this timber has the right weight; it never twists on its shank; and it can be given the true 'striking' angle, an angle which will never change, even though the centre of the striking face may, with the passage of years, become delicately indented through continuous impact with the beech handles of innumerable chisels and gouges.

It is this quality of toughness and hardness, the result of close and fine grain, that has made beech a favourite timber with the makers of a vast number of smallish objects that have to be able to withstand impact or heavy pressure in various ways. Most rolling-pins are made of beech; many bread boards are made of specially selected beech. The vices on many joiners' benches, even today, are often equipped with boards and screws of beech: the joiner will tell you that a wooden grip is kinder to the surfaces of the timber he is working on than a metal one can ever be. Many of these vice screws are as accurately cut out of beech as any steel screw could be, and after years of use retain their sharp edges and run as true as they did on the day they came from the turner's lathe.

If you examine the chopping-blocks and tables in any butcher's shop, the chances are that they will prove to be made of a great number of small, rectangular blocks of beech set with their end-grain uppermost and clamped together with heavy iron clamps at each corner. Such blocks will stand up to the keen edges of the butcher's knives and the heavy weight of his cleavers and show hardly any sign of wear at all. Gradually, though, after years of use, and week-end scrubbing with stiff-bristled brushes, these chopping-blocks acquire curious and pleasing contours, like a miniature landscape eroded by rain and wind and frost.

Most brushes and broom heads, whether small nail brushes or big street-cleaners' brooms, are made of half-rounds of beech. There is a good reason for this: its close, fine grain enables the wood to take a great number of close-set bristle holes without splitting. If you turn a brush or broom over and examine the holes closely you will see that they are often practically touching, being 'staggered' slightly to enable as many bristles as possible to be in contact. Only beech could stand up to this sort of perforation, and it is probable that almost any brush you look at, whatever form of outer covering or veneer it may have been given, is a piece of beech wood.

The craftsmen working in beech were regularly called upon by the country bakers to make their 'peels'—the very long handled beech shovels which they used for raking out their loaves from the back of their big brick ovens. Some of these country bakers still use such peels today, and it is probably not mere imagination that makes one believe that bread baked in such ovens, handled by beechwood peels, is tastier and more appetizing than the machine-made bread turned out in millions of loaves by the big, soulless, multiple bakeries.

Maltsters, too, use big shovels for stirring their malt, and for these their choice is always beech. The 'mushrooms' housewives use when darning socks are usually made of beech: the mushroom-like top will be smooth enough for use with silk, and hard enough to withstand the prick of the needle without splintering; and the handle can be not only turned to a convenient size for a woman's hand, but hollowed out to hold a few spare needles, and take a good thread that enables it to be screwed into the top without the risk of its ever working loose.

Though sycamore is sometimes used, the lasts on which the best boots and shoes are made, and the 'trees' on which they are often kept in order to preserve their shape and prevent wrinkles

CLOG MAKER'S
'STOCK-KNIFE'

and cracks, are usually of beech, which can be fashioned as delicately as clay can be modelled by a skilled potter.

The shaping of these lasts and trees is done with quite an armoury of differently curved knives, for the proportions will be those of the human foot itself. Some of these knives are used also by the craftsman who specializes in the making of clogs— or, in France, the wooden sabot, which is often made of beech. One of the most important of his tools is known as a 'stock-knife'. This is a longish blade, the lower end of which is fitted to a swivel on the craftsman's bench. When he is working he holds the block of beech in one hand, turning it about deftly and bringing to bear on it the long, keen edge of his stock-knife, which he manipulates with his other hand.

There are not many of these craftsmen to be seen today. But if you happen to be off the beaten track, particularly in some parts of Lancashire, you may come across a clog maker seated at his bench in a shed at the back of his cottage, or even in a back room of his cottage, his feet and lower legs deep in curling white shavings and a growing pile of clog soles rising beside him, much as the trug maker builds up his product while he sits in front of his 'horse'. The stock-knife is wielded with extraordinary skill and precision and the white shavings flutter down on to the bench, and eventually on to the floor, in a steady stream, like goose feathers from a bird that is being dextrously plucked by a farmer's wife! When the piece has been cut to the approximately right shape by the swivelling stock-knife, the clog maker takes up one or other of his keen-edged and curiously shaped smaller tools and finishes it off in detail with these.

Another worker in beech who is still to be found carrying on a tradition somewhere between the Chiltern chair bodger and the very humble gipsy clothes-peg maker is the maker of tent pegs. Though the beech-wood tent peg is somewhat heavier and bulkier that the modern aluminium-alloy tent peg now so much in demand by lightweight campers and holiday-makers, it is impossible to beat for general efficiency in holding guy-ropes against strong wind and the immense strain of ropes pulled taut by changes of humidity. Because it is comparatively small, the tent peg can be made out of pieces of beech that would be of little use for other purposes.

Tent pegs are made in enormous numbers, often by gangs of men who take on a contract for many thousands of them at a time and set up their simple workshops among the beech trees exactly as the chair bodgers have always done. They use the same type of primitive 'bench'—a tree stump driven into the ground and levelled off at a height convenient for the individual craftsman to work on. On this he cleaves the short lengths of beech that have been cross-cut to the measurements required; and when the last of his boles of beech have been cleft and turned into pegs, he will probably cleave the bench itself and make a final bundle of pegs out of that, so that nothing is wasted!

The beech is invariably cleft, not sawn—though cheap, mass-produced pegs are in fact on sale in some shops; you will discover for yourself whether you have bought the genuine article or not the very first time you pick up a mallet to knock it into the ground. The sawn variety will almost certainly split at the first blow of your mallet; the other will 'keep its head'.

With a small axe, or mallet and froe, the peg maker will cleave his beech to a suitable thickness in readiness for shaping and trimming. If the pegs he is to make are of the smaller size he may simplify his task by driving a piece of iron into the top of his bench, filing it to an edge, and doing his cleaving by tapping each piece of wood downwards on to it so that the cleft wood falls automatically apart. Then he picks up his draw-knife and quickly tapers the wood to the right angle on its inner edge to enable it to enter the ground easily under the impact of the mallet. With a sharp knife or, in the case of the larger pegs, a small saw blade, he cuts a 'nick' into the edge just above the taper, and slants that away so as to give a grip for the guy rope or canvas eyelet, carefully trimming the under-edge of this nick in order to minimize the wear-and-tear when the peg is in use. One last refinement before the pegs are stacked criss-cross, like the chair legs, to season: the head of each peg has its four edges lightly bevelled. This not only makes the peg look better

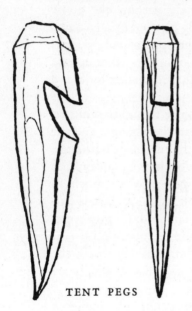

TENT PEGS

'finished', but prevents it from splaying outwards under the mallet's impact.

Curiously, though beech is so hard, and so resistant to warping, it can be very easily steam-bent, and having once been bent to shape it will retain that shape indefinitely. The chair commonly known as a 'bentwood' chair, seen in cafés and village halls and elsewhere, is made almost entirely of beech. A beech pole about an inch in thickness or rather more—the thickness, say, of a broom handle—is steamed and then bent into an open circle, the two ends being continued downwards to form the pair of back legs for the chair. The front legs, as is the case with the Windsor chair, will also be of beech, though not adorned with the rings that belong to that older type of chair, and will be very slightly splayed outwards. The heavier ring into which the circular perforated or 'pressed' seat is inset will also be of beech, likewise the stay which curves across the back in some of the more substantial models. But though it is extremely light and flimsy looking, the bentwood chair is remarkably strong and will take the weight of a grown man even if he tilts it backwards at a considerable angle.

Beech is the first choice of the country saddler. Not when he is making his light riding-saddles but when he is at work on the massive type that carries the heavy chain supporting the shafts of a waggon or cart. This is more usually known as a 'pad', and the careful owner of a cart-horse will always see to it that the pad it wears is made to measure.

Its main feature is a grooved arch over which the chain passes. It needs to be very carefully designed so that it is at once strong enough for the job it is intended to perform and not an ounce heavier than it has to be, since the horse has to carry it as well as the chain and the considerable weight of the shafts. Beech is ideal for this, since it is easy to carve and resistant to wear and stresses in any direction. On to it there is built an elaborate covering of upholstery and stout leather, probably adorned with brass-headed nails. It may not have the subtle curves and sheen

93

of a riding-saddle, but it will fit the broad back of the cart-horse perfectly and distribute the weight of the shafts evenly and fairly.

Other country craftsmen using beech turned to it for a blend of two important qualities. Sieves, barrels to hold 'dry goods', gallon measures and other containers of the kind for corn and other grain, were made of beech, because it could be easily steambent to shape and would retain its shape no matter how much the articles might be knocked about in farmyards, grain stores, village shops, and so on. Children's hoops were made of beech, though it is very rare to see one in use today. The rims of bandsmen's drums, curiously enough, are still very often made of beech hoops skilfully shaped, then steamed and finally trimmed again by craftsmen with long years of this sort of work behind them and the skill now ingrained in their fingertips.

In fact, when you come to consider it, beech combines a number of qualities that you would hardly expect to find in one timber. It is almost as rigid as well-seasoned oak, yet it is almost as pliant as willow; it has a grain so delicate that it is a timber easy to work with the simple pole lathe and a handful of chisels and gouges, or even a sharp knife. The grain is such that the finished article, large or small, looks attractive and feels attractive too. Its one weakness lies in the fact that, generally speaking, beech does not stand up well to use out of doors, or in fact to contact with anything wet.

In spite of this, however, so popular was it indoors that country craftsmen, and housewives too, succeeded in finding ways of making beechwood utensils stand up to the effects of the liquids they were made to contain. One of these was to 'smoke' the beechwood of which bowls and platters were turned; another was to allow hot mutton fat to soak into its pores over and over again! There are such utensils to be seen in cottages today that have served several generations of their owners and are likely to serve many generations more.

Craftsmen in Ash

ASH carries the proud title of 'Our Toughest Timber'. It is the timber Man has always turned to when he required not so much the weight and sheer strength of oak as something that combined lightness, pliancy, ease of manipulation and resistance to stress with strength and the power to retain its shape however great the demands placed upon it. Ash has all these qualities.

The Romans knew this two thousand years ago. Not long ago an iron implement was unearthed in their settlement in Caerleon, Monmouthshire. In its iron socket was a short stump of wood. When experts analysed it they found that it was ash: the remains of an ash handle fitted by some Roman craftsman to the work of some Roman blacksmith.

From then onwards ash was in constant demand. The lances of the Crusaders and the knights who fought in tournaments were steel-tipped ash shafts; the pikes and halberds of the medieval soldier had ash shafts; the pitchforks used by farmers throughout the centuries have always had shafts of ash: they possessed lightness combined with strength, and enough 'whip' to enable a man to toss a heavy bundle of hay or a couple of sheaves of corn from ground level on to a waggon, or from the waggon on to the rick, with little more than a deft flick of his wrist and jerk of his elbow.

One of the very valuable qualities of this timber is its extraordinary ability to stand up to sudden and violent strain or shock without 'shivering', or having its strength and pliancy in the slightest degree weakened. It is for this reason that the miner's pick invariably has a haft of ash. It will take the violent shock of the impact of pick point on coal face over and over again through-out the whole of the miner's stint, and go on doing this for days and weeks and months. The point of the pick will become blunt and have to be sharpened; the metal may even crack or splinter; but the haft will outlast several replacements of head, and remain as strong as it was when its first head was put on to it.

The quarryman's and blacksmith's sledge-hammers—four-pounders, seven-pounders and fourteen-pounders—are all fitted with hafts of ash. The woodman's axe—whether it is the big two-handed felling-axe or the smaller barking-axe or shingle axe or handy chopper or hatchet—will have a haft of ash. The maul, or 'beetle', or 'biddle', used with a set of wedges for cleaving tree trunks or slate or other stone, will have a haft of ash. Forks, rakes, shovels, spades, shepherds' crooks—almost every long-handled implement in use in farm or garden, in forestry or market-gardening, in quarrying or other heavy industry, on the railways for shunters' poles and countless other uses—must be fitted with hafts of ash. It possesses a toughness and strength that make it the first choice for all such purposes. Curiously enough, we use the phrase 'tough as hickory'; yet it remains a fact that if a woodman has the choice between American hickory and English ash for the hafts of his axes, he never hesitates: it is ash every time. And this goes for the miner and quarryman too.

It is therefore not surprising that ash should play an important part in the world of sport. Gymnasium parallel-bars and horizon-tal-bars are made of ash; cricket-stumps, billiard-cues, hockey-sticks, croquet-mallets, baseball-bats, polo-clubs, tennis-rackets, skis, snow-shoes, sledge-runners, oars and paddles and a hundred other items of sport equipment large and small are made of ash, and many sportsmen still prefer this to the tubular light alloys that are being experimented with today for such purposes, success-ful as they often are.

Among the finest craftsmen using ash are the wheelwrights. The wheelwright, of course, is not concerned only with the making of wheels, though this may be the most highly specialized aspect of his craft. He is an expert carpenter and joiner, and he and his assistants will between them build a waggon or cart or other road vehicle complete from start to finish. He will use a variety of timbers for his work, but foremost among them will be ash, since he knows from long experience that there is no other timber with such qualities for certain purposes. The 'felloes' of his wheels will be of ash; and the shafts, too, as well as parts of the framework.

Shafts of course vary enormously in weight and in design, according to the type of vehicle to which they are to be fitted. But one feature is all-important: they must be perfectly matched, off-side and near-side, in every respect. Because they need to be very strong in relation to their weight, whenever it is possible they will be cut from a tree, or bough, that has some slight approximation to the finished article. A good wheelwright, or the timber merchant from whom he buys his oak, beech, elm and ash, will be constantly on the lookout for trees that may lend themselves to his needs. In this he resembles the old shipwright, who 'grew' his oak in such a way that it would supply not only stem-posts and stern-posts, but ribs and knees that he would be able to turn to good account when he started building. If, as you go about the countryside, you keep an eye cocked towards the ash trees, which often grow isolated from their fellows in the middle of fields, you may be able to spot the sort of stem or main bough likeliest to be of use to the wheelwright for a pair of heavy shafts.

The essential thing is that there should be at any rate a suggestion of a curve at the point at which the curve would appear in the completed shafts. Shafts are normally shaped with curves in two 'planes': the major curve is the one that accommodates the bulk of the horse working between them; the lesser curve will be outwards and downwards at the point at which the collar is attached. The curves can, of course, be, and very often are, put into the timber by the wheelwright; but he much prefers to make use of timber that already has a hint of the final curve, as it were 'built into' it by nature.

Having selected his stem, or bough, and cut it to length, the craftsman takes up his 'snap-line'. This consists of two pegs, which he drives into the timber, one at each end, and a length of twine which he either rubs with chalk or soaks in a mixture of wax and lamp-black, then stretches between the pegs and 'snaps' down on

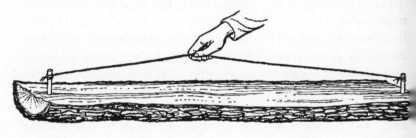

SHAFT MAKER'S 'SNAP-LINE'

the timber beneath it. In this way, however rough the surface of the timber, he obtains an absolutely straight line from end to end. It is along this line that he will saw, and when the two halves fall apart he will have a pair of embryo shafts identical in curve and thickness and weight. It remains then to get to work on them first with a light axe, then with a draw-knife and finally with a spokeshave, whittling away all superfluous wood and emphasizing the curves, whether concave or convex, tapering the shaft from the heavy end, which will be attached to the waggon or cart, to the far end, on to which he will later put the traditional brass ferrule.

If you examine a pair of finished shafts carefully you will see that the 'section' varies throughout their length. At the heavy end it will be either square or rectangular; this allows plenty of room for driving through it the heavy bolts which will attach it to the framework of the cart or to the hinges that will allow it to rise and fall from the swivelling fore-part of a waggon. Where the shafts curve outwards to accommodate the belly of the horse the section will have changed a good deal. It will probably be straight sided on the outward side, bevelled or chamfered at the outer corners, and very smoothly curved on the inner side to avoid chafing the horse's coat. The taper will be continued uniformly throughout, and the wheelwright will remove as much wood as he dares, because shafts are 'dead weight' and the horse has to carry this slung over its back by the chain riding over the 'pad'. It must have enough strength to hold rigid the various staples and hooks and other metal fittings necessary for the harness-work, but every ounce that can be removed means that much less 'dead weight' for the horse to carry.

It is details such as these that the craftsman must bear constantly in mind as he works. In all probability he has no list of written measurements: he has been at his trade long enough to be able to visualize the finished pair of shafts while he is still in the initial stages and working on the roughly trimmed ash. The shafts, when completed, must not only match perfectly in their proportions but be identical in weight; otherwise they will be out of balance and that will affect the pulling-powers of the horse that is to work between them.

Ash is used elsewhere in cart and waggon making because it possesses the ideal combination of qualities: strength, resilience and lightness. It will withstand the continuous pounding that results from rough surfaces beneath the wheels and the transport of heavy, bulky and often unwieldy loads. It has the notable quality of 'giving' to a minute but still sufficient extent, and reverting to its true shape and rigidity after each impact or shock or strain. Its elasticity and toughness constitute an ideal combination.

This is particularly desirable in the wheel itself. Though, as we have already seen, the spokes will be made of heart of oak, and, as we shall see, the hub, or 'stock', will be made of elm, the 'felloes'—the short curved pieces of which the rim of the wheel is built up—will be of ash, on to which the wheelwright and his fellow craftsman, the blacksmith, will shrink an iron tyre to bind the whole together.

The wheel, naturally, has to possess great strength, for it is 'dead weight' and takes all the shock of road surface transmitted upwards to the load that is being carried; though the framework of the cart or waggon in some cases has springs to cushion it and its contents from shock, the wheel has none at all. This is one reason why more and more carts and waggons today are being fitted with metal wheels and big-section rubber tyres: they ease the load and wear-and-tear on the waggon; they reduce the strain on the cart-horse; but they spell the gradual end of the craft of wheelwrighting—one of the finest and noblest of all country crafts.

As you might expect, ash is the timber used for most ladders, certainly for the best ladders. Firemen's ladders, in particular, unless they are made of some light alloy, are made of ash: no ladder serves a more vital purpose than the firemen's ladders do.

The ladder maker selects his ash with the utmost care, making sure that it is as knot-free as possible, as straight as possible, and with a good, even grain. Using his 'snap-line', he cleaves his ash pole down the dead centre and then, if he finds any unsuspected knots, or 'shakes', lays the timber on one side for some less important purpose and looks for a better pole. Having cleft a length of ash and found it satisfactory, he proceeds to lay his snap-line down the flat inner surface, first of one and then of the other half, and 'snap' out a dead-straight line for the rung holes. He is of course very careful to see that every ladder he makes comes from the same pole; otherwise there might be a slight difference in weight, and this would mean a ladder that was sub-standard. It is as important to have the two halves perfectly matched as it is to have the two shafts a perfect pair, from the same piece of timber.

Having got his two lines marked out on the inner surfaces of his half-rounds of ash, which he has previously trimmed smooth with draw-knife and spokeshave, he bores holes at intervals of nine inches from one end to the other, being careful to work from both butt ends outwards. The holes are bored with a brace and bit of the right size, and then slightly tapered with an auger so as to make a snug fit over the tapered ends of the rungs, or 'staves'.

One of the ladder lengths is then laid, flat side upwards, on a series of low trestles all of exactly equal height, and the oak staves tapped firmly into the holes so that they project by a fraction of an inch downwards on the rounded side. These projections will of course be smoothed away when the two sides have been assembled and the final stages of trimming are begun. The half-round with its staves, resembling a giant comb, is then laid on its side and the other half-round brought close to it on the trestles. The stave ends are lightly tapped into the row of waiting holes and then the two ladder sides are pressed firmly together by laying across them a number of screw, or 'sash', clamps and tightening these progressively more and more all the way along.

This may sound a very simple process indeed, but in fact it calls for a high degree of skill in the craftsman. Except for some types of extending ladders, all ladders taper somewhat from base to summit. This taper may be only a matter of three or four inches spread over a length of twenty or thirty or more feet; but it must be absolutely consistent throughout the length of the ladder. The ladder maker, who has prepared his oak staves with this in mind, each one fractionally shorter than the one before it, working from the base outwards, has to compress the ladder sides uniformly in such a way that the tightness of every separate stave is identical with every one before and after it. This calls for an accuracy of eye and a sense of judgment of a very high order indeed.

In certain parts of the country, notably in fruit-picking districts such as those of Kent and Worcestershire, ladders of a special type are always in demand. They have more 'splay' than the standard ladders made for window-cleaners, builders, firemen and others need have. The splay may amount to several feet at the base of the ladder, which will enable the fruit picker to lean well out of equilibrium when he is among the upper branches of a tree, and yet not come tumbling to the ground. But it involves elaborate calculation on the part of the ladder maker. The sides of his ladder may be straight or slightly curved, but his stave lengths will vary much more than those of the standard ladder, and the holes he bores into the ladder sides will, at the splayed end, have to be bored at a difficult angle so that the staves remain parallel to the ground even though they must pierce the ladder sides on the slant. These are angles which the ladder maker produces by feel and instinct rather than by mechanical means.

The finished ladder must be in perfect balance. He must have trimmed each half-round so that there is not an ounce of difference between the weight of one and that of the other. The 'splay', if any, must be identical; the taper of the standard ladder exactly proportioned. Because the user's hands will run up and down the outside of the half-rounds, these must be absolutely smooth, the stave ends rounded off flush with the grain so that they cannot be felt at all. Luckily ash takes on a very smooth finish indeed, and very rarely splinters whatever treatment it receives—another of its many useful qualities.

Though ladder making is done from half-rounds, ash generally is very little used 'in the round'. For most of the innumerable purposes for which it is the chosen timber of the craftsman he prefers quick-grown ash poles that are between twenty and thirty years old. The wheelwright and coach-builder, of course, must use older timber, since bulkier pieces are required for shafts and framework. The smaller objects are almost invariably made from cleft ash that has had the pith and sapwood removed so that what remains is of prime quality.

Naturally cleft ash is always chosen for the making of handles —the hafts—usually known to the craftsman as 'stails'—of picks and sledge-hammers and axes and so on. It will often be found that communities of craftsmen specializing in this work have sprung up and maintained a long tradition in localities where their products are continuously in demand. They are to be found, for instance, within hail of the South Wales coalfields and of the foundries and steelworks of Sheffield and the Black Country, where fine ash hafts are essential to men working with heavy, wooden-handled tools.

Straight and quick-grown ash poles are first cross-cut to approximately the right length for the purpose for which they are designed. Then, using axe, beetle and fromard and working on a chopping-block, the craftsman cleaves his pole into conveniently sized segments of approximately square section. Next, he mounts his roughly shaped timber on a bench that is solid, massive and practical. It consists of little more than a heavy timber shelf with a slot cut in its near side. At one end of the slot a fixed wooden block holds a steel spike; a corresponding steel spike projects from another wooden block set in the slot in such a way that it can be moved towards or from the fixed block and then securely locked in position at the right distance.

Between these two steel spikes the length of ash is mounted horizontally, though it can be turned on its long axis to suit the convenience of the craftsman. Using a selection of draw-knives and spokeshaves, some with straight, some with curved blades and all exceedingly sharp, he quickly transforms the rough baulk of ash into the finished product.

Sledge-hammer hafts, of course, are perfectly straight, slightly oval in section, and usually without any taper at all. Axe hafts, on the other hand, are very elaborately shaped and therefore demand a great deal more time in their making, and the highest degree of skill and patience in the craftsman.

If you examine an axe haft, whether it belongs to a big two-handed felling-axe or a small hatchet, you will see that the curves in it are identical in proportion throughout and differ only in their size according to the length of the different hafts. There is a double curve; or indeed a triple curve. The curve of an axe haft corresponds surprisingly closely to that of the human backbone— as you will realize if you ever look at a skeleton. It begins just below the head, at the neck, and curves downwards by way of the shoulders to the waist; then the curve changes again, swinging a

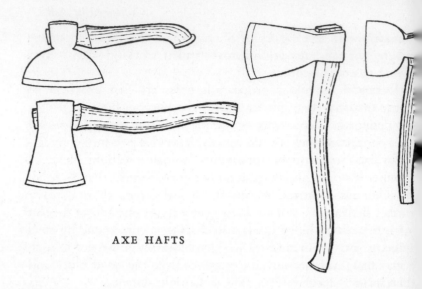

AXE HAFTS

little outwards, and then inwards to the point on the human backbone where once we had a tail.

Follow the curve through on the axe, and the proportions are very much the same. The end of the haft penetrates the head, or blade, of the axe. There is a sort of shoulder just below the point at which the haft enters the head. Then the curve runs very slightly inwards, in the direction of the edge of the blade, and midway down begins to run outwards again to balance the first curve and bring the axis of the haft in line with the centre of the head. Then once again the curve changes as it reaches the point at which the user's hand will grasp it—the hand that remains fixed, while the other slides up and down the haft. Here it thickens considerably, to afford anchorage for the hand. This beautifully calculated swelling at the end of the haft is known to the craftsman who made it as the 'fawn's foot', and it is a most apt name for it as you will immediately realize when you examine it. It is calculated to prevent the user's hand from slipping off the end of the haft when the axe is at the maximum of its upward or downward swing.

Why is it that an axe haft should have this elaborately curved shape to it? The shape it has today is the shape it has had for hundreds of years, and will never be altered because long experience among hundreds of thousands of users has shown that it is the best that could be devised. And the interesting thing about it is that it derives from the primitive axe handle that was used by prehistoric Man when he searched for flints in the chalk of the Sussex Downs and the quarries of Grimes Graves on the Suffolk-Norfolk border. You can see this for yourself if you go to any museum where such objects have been put on show.

For the earliest tools of this kind were the antlers of certain deer. If you look at some of these close to, and particularly if you happen already to have a good idea of what an axe haft looks like today, you will see that the curves and proportions are almost identical in all of them. Every axe that has been made since Man began to make, instead of adapt, these implements, has been given a handle based on that ancient and excellent pattern.

The craftsman making axe hafts today is very highly skilled indeed. For not only must he give his piece of ash the right curves, and in their right proportions; he must also vary the thickness and the 'section' of the ash continuously, from head to 'fawn's foot'. It will be long and narrow and wedge-shaped at the end which penetrates the blade, and a saw-cut down its long axis will take a long, thin, tapering metal or hardwood wedge to secure the head in position and prevent it from flying off when it is swung by the user. It will have wood at the shoulder, but the size of the section, both lengthwise and across, will diminish, and the proportions of the oval change, as the curve continues downwards to the midway point. Then the thickness of the haft will increase slightly as it is curved back to the point at which the user's 'fixed' hand will grasp it, swelling to the beautifully proportioned heel, or fawn's foot, at the very end.

All these continuously changing curves and proportions have to be borne in mind by the craftsman. He works, of course, from a piece of ash that is rectangular in section rather than square, so that he can obtain his inward and outward curves from it. He knows all the time, as he applies his draw-knife or spokeshave, that whereas he can always cut away a little more wood, if he has once cut away too much, he can never put it back. Like a chess player, he must work all the time a 'move' or two ahead of what he is doing. A row of graduated axe hafts, suspended from the ceiling of a country ironmonger's or hardware merchant's shop, presents a pattern of graceful curves which would be hard to beat among any man-made objects in any other field of activity.

Owing to the ease with which ash can be manipulated, it is the favourite timber for the elaborately curved scythe handle, known to the craftsman as the 'snead', or 'snaith'. Unlike the axe haft, this is round in section throughout, though it is gradually tapered from the point at which the blade is attached to the other end. Very occasionally a snaith is made from a young ash sapling; but almost all of them, and certainly the best of them, are made from cleft ash poles with the grain left intact and the pith and sapwood carefully removed.

The preliminary shaping of the ash is done, as usual, with axe, beetle and fromard. Then, because the curves a scythe snaith must possess are far more pronounced than those of an axe, the roughly prepared pole must be bent to shape, and this involves steaming to make it sufficiently pliant. Having steamed his length of ash until it is malleable, the craftsman takes it to his oddly named 'setting-pin'. This is actually a much bigger and more elaborate affair than its name suggests. It consists of a massive wooden post driven deep into the ground or the floor of his workshop and possessing a number of metal or hardwood 'jaws' of different sizes and angles. Through these the craftsman pushes his pliant ash pole, exerting pressure on it as he does so in various directions and with varying degrees of strength, until the snaith has been given the necessary curves—curves which are of course, in two or more 'planes', not in one only.

When the snaith has been given the necessary curves it is quickly removed from the last of the setting-pin jaws and laid across a bench consisting of a number of heavy baulks of timber

SNAITH MAKER'S 'SETTING-PIN'

laid horizontally and containing a number of hardwood pegs driven into holes in their upper surfaces at carefully calculated points. Each snaith as it comes from the setting-pin is laid across these baulks of timber, in and out of the hardwood pegs, in such a way that it is held rigid while the heat and moisture depart from it. Once they are cold and dry, the snaiths can be removed and will retain their artificially induced curves indefinitely.

The next process is to trim the snaith. It must be perfectly round in section and uniformly tapered from the butt end to the top end. The butt end is shaped something like a pony's hoof: there must be plenty of wood there for the bolt, clip or other device which holds the blade in position; enough, too, to grip the wedges that will be driven through the collar to make the blade rigid. From that point upwards the snaith will diminish considerably in diameter until it is perhaps little more than the thickness of a man's thumb at the extremity.

To produce this uniform taper and roundness of section the craftsman uses a curious and rather primitive-looking tool which he refers to as a 'stail-engine'. It consists of a block of wood into

SNAITH MAKER'S
'STAIL-ENGINE'

which two keen blades are set at an angle to one another and facing inwards, each capable of adjustment. The craftsman grasps his tool in both hands and works it spirally along the snaith, tightening it at intervals so that it shrinks on to the wood and produces the required taper as it does so. This is the final stage in the shaping of the snaith.

All that remains now to be done is to attach the two short handles, known as 'snees', or 'doles', each of which can be very simply adjusted when the time comes to use the scythe. The blade will be supplied separately, and in all probability 'set' on the snaith, as will the two 'doles', by the man who is going to use it. For a scythe is about as individual an implement as any to be found in the whole armoury of country workers' tools and no two men will agree exactly as to the right angle of the blade or the position of the handles.

The 'stail-engine' is sometimes used also for the trimming of the long handles, or 'stails', on hay rakes. These, since they do not need to have great strength, are often cut from young stems, their bark roughly trimmed away and a certain degree of roundness given to them by this handy if clumsy-looking tool. A slight unevenness in a hay rake handle does not matter in the least, and indeed helps to prevent it from becoming greasy and slippery with sweat. It will probably not be absolutely straight. In fact, many farm workers prefer a rake handle that has a slight curve in it to begin with, as this tends to flatten out with use as the rake settles in their hands.

The head of the hay rake will be of ash also: a piece sawn or cleft and roughly trimmed to rectangular section with a draw-knife and then pierced with a number of holes. There are usually fifteen of these, set about two inches apart. Into these the rake maker drives cleft ash pegs about five inches long, an inch of which will be in the rake head itself. Sometimes the pegs are very roughly trimmed to triangular or square section before being driven into the holes prepared for them; alternatively each cleft peg is driven through a piece of iron piping with a sharpened edge in such a way as to trim it automatically to fit the hole. Each peg is then trimmed to a blunt point, the craftsman using what he calls a 'peg-knife', which resembles the clog maker's 'stock-knife' in being secured by a swivel to his bench with the upper end free to be manipulated in any direction.

The thicker end of the stail is sawn down the middle for about eighteen inches or a couple of feet and the two halves are then forced apart after the top of the saw-cut has been bound with a narrow ring of tin exactly as the gipsy binds his willow clothes-pegs to prevent them from splitting. The two halves are then tapered slightly at the tips and tapped into two holes bored about eight inches or so apart in the side of the head. They are tapped well home, and if necessary secured with a couple of wire nails or small pegs driven through the head across the grain. These will ensure that the head remains fast to the stail however hard the user drags on it when raking hay. If, however, it does work a little loose, he drops it into a water trough for a few minutes and the wood then swells sufficiently for the original fit to be regained. If it is still too loose, the nails are tapped through, the head is

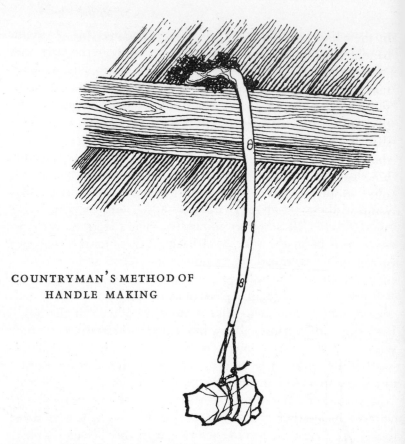

COUNTRYMAN'S METHOD OF
HANDLE MAKING

driven a little further on to the tapered ends of the stail, and the
fit is then as good as ever.

Though ash generally is not much used 'in the round', there
is one use for young saplings in which cleaving has no place at all.
This is in the making of walking-sticks. It is true that the countryman usually cuts his stick straight from any coppice as soon as he
sees one that he likes the look of. It may be hazel, or thorn, or
ash, or chestnut, or indeed any one of a number of different woods.
If he wants a handle to it, either curved or angled, he will suspend
his stick from a beam in his cottage, or in a barn, with the thick
end locked in a cranny, and fasten a weight to the lower end.

In the course of time sheer gravity will have produced a crook
handle to his liking: it is as simple as that!

But walking-sticks are required in great numbers by holiday-
makers, and there is a walking-stick 'factory' in a Surrey village
where the craftsmen work much as their fellow craftsmen do in
the trug-making village of Herstmonceux, across the border,
shaping natural materials with very simple tools. The two woods
they mainly use are chestnut and ash, though there are people
who send them all sorts of individual lengths of other woods,
often exotic woods from far-flung corners of the world, with a
request that they will shape them to their needs.

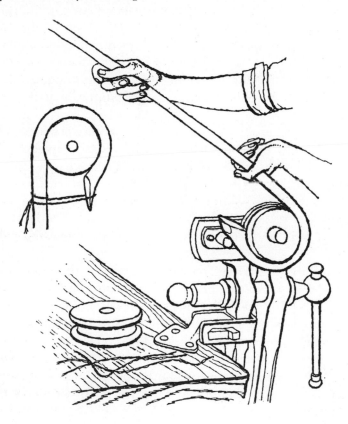

BENDING WALKING-STICK HANDLES

All chestnut and many ash poles are given curved handles. The stems are cut from Surrey coppices and brought in bundles into the workshop, where deep trays of coarse, dark sand are kept constantly heated by ovens beneath them. Into these trays of sand the stems, having been first cut to length, are plunged, till they look like the quills in a porcupine stretched round three sides of the room.

When they have been heated sufficiently to become malleable they are removed from the sand and the first of two processes is quickly undertaken. Using a solid wooden 'horse' closely resembling the 'setting-pin' of the snaith maker, the craftsman 'irons out' the kinks in the sticks. Each stick is passed between one pair of pegs and given a slight wrench in one direction or the other; the result is very quickly a die-straight stem not unlike a billiard-cue. The hot sand has temporarily taken the 'nature' out of the wood. While it is in this condition it is easy to straighten it; and when the stick has cooled, and its 'nature' returned to it, it is set for life.

The second process is to give the stick its curved handle. Once again the heat is applied; this time, however, by plunging the thicker end of the stick into hot water. When it has become soft enough it is removed, bent quickly round a grooved iron ring and tied into that position with a piece of strong twine deftly slipped over it and pulled tight. By the time it has cooled it will have set in its semi-circular curve, and it will retain this indefinitely.

More to the true walker's taste, however, than any crook-handled stick of chestnut or even ash is what is commonly known as the 'ash-plant', though this is technically known as a 'cross-head ash'. This has a knobby, solid head at right angles to the stem which gives it a 'character' that no crook-handled chestnut or ash stick can ever possess. You will never see any two exactly alike. This, of course, is one reason for the popularity of the ash-plant; another is its strength, and the 'feel' of it within the hand that uses it.

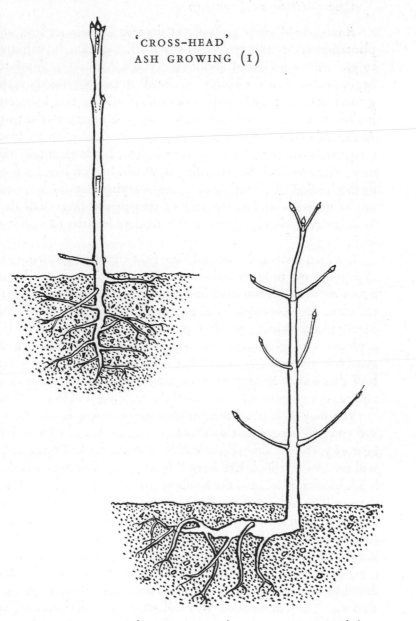

'CROSS-HEAD'
ASH GROWING (I)

'CROSS-HEAD' ASH GROWING (2)

A cross-head ash is grown, not shaped. The ash sapling, in a plantation as carefully tended as any market-garden, is permitted to grow for a period of about two years. As soon as any buds begin to appear on the stem these are all picked off, exactly as the grower of cricket-bat willow prunes his trees. One bud, however, is allowed to continue to grow; it is the one nearest to the root. At the end of the two-year growth period the sapling is lifted from the ground and the root alone is replanted, but horizontally this time, with the single bud pointing upwards. It is left like this for a further period of about three years—varying slightly with the rate of growth—and at the end of that period there will be a straight stem rather longer than the standard length of a walking-stick.

It is then uprooted a second time (not cut off at ground level, of course), and brought indoors to have the hot sand and 'horse' treatment that will eliminate any kinks that may have grown into the stem. Any knots left by the constant trimming away of buds during its three-year period of growth are then smoothed by the application of glass-paper on a revolving 'buffer'; a touch of varnish is given to any wood that is bare of the thin, grey-green bark that is such an attractive feature of an ash-plant; a ferrule is tapped on to the thinner end—and the walking-stick is complete.

You may look at a thousand such sticks—'cross-head ashes'—and you will never find two that have identical heads. There will be stocky, chunky ones; there will be straight, thickish ones; there will be ones that look like horses' heads, dogs' heads, crocodiles' heads, elephants' heads—the heads of any animal real or fabulous; there will be heads that tempt you to pull out your penknife and begin to 'finish them off' into the semblance of something they remind you of, and you will drive in a couple of brown glass-headed pins and give your stick a name. And unless you do something drastic with it, your ash-plant will outlast the lives of half a dozen ferrules and stand you in good stead for as long as you go walking. The connoisseur will collect a new ash-plant every year, and build up a 'menagerie' of them, each with a character of its own and a name to which it may almost be expected to answer!

Cleft, or 'in the round'—though mostly the former—ash is a country craftsman's timber. Whether it is used for making shafts, for wheel felloes, for coach frames, ladder sides, pick handles, axe hafts, halberds or hay rakes, or for little tools—the gardener's trowel and weeding-fork, his shears or 'dibbers' or anything else—or for walking-sticks, 'shinty-sticks', cattle-drovers' heavy sticks, barrel hoops or anything else of the kind, ash responds to the divers needs of the man who handles it or is to make use of the finished article. It is tough, versatile, enduring, and at the same time amenable to discipline. Of no other timber can all this be said without any reservations; and in no other timber does the craftsman's art show to greater advantage.

Craftsmen in Straw and Reed

WHEN primitive Man first began to build himself a house, instead of remaining content with the security of a cave, he had to find something suitable for a roof. It had to be strong enough to stand up to wind and weather, thick enough to protect him from snow and rain, yet light enough to be supported by the sort of walls he was capable of building. He found that heather, ling, turf, brushwood and so on was admirable for his purpose, and made use of them for many hundreds of years. In the remote parts of Ireland, the Western Isles of Scotland, and elsewhere you will often come across low-built dwellings with turf and brushwood roofs that have hardly changed in any way from those that were the early experiments of primitive Man.

Straw and reed, however, have almost entirely replaced the earlier types of material today. The men who make roofs, whether for buildings or for ricks, are thatchers: craftsmen whose days are numbered because other farming methods are replacing the old and well-tried methods, and not many people go in for thatch for the roofs of their houses. It is rare to find a thatcher who is not middle-aged or elderly; it is very rare indeed to find a young man taking up the craft. 'There's no future in thatching,' would be the answer, if you asked him why.

The work of the thatcher is seen at its best in the West Country and in East Anglia, where the tradition has remained longest and strongest. Now and then you will come across thatched buildings in other parts of the country. For the most part they are old ones —cottages, barns, farmhouses and the like—on which the old thatch has clung longer than usual, or maybe the owner has succeeded in finding a thatcher who is prepared to leave his district and come and work on one building at any rate in a new district before returning to the part of the country where he has operated perhaps for the better part of a long lifetime.

Though it is of course true to say that all craftsmen are to a greater or a lesser extent individualists, with a 'personal' touch in their work which is as tell-tale of their individuality as the finger-prints are of a suspect criminal, probably the thatcher is more of an individual even than most. Almost alone among craftsmen, he works as an isolated figure. Though chair bodgers, clothes-peg makers, lobster-pot makers, hurdle makers and others usually work in small groups, or even in whole communities, it is rare to see more than one thatcher at work at a time on a roof; at best he will have an assistant preparing his straw or reed down at the foot of the ladder and carrying it up to keep him well supplied. He is as solitary a figure as the dowser, and works 'up aloft' for almost every hour of his working life.

In the days when there were great numbers of thatched roofs in almost all parts of the country, the expert in such matters could usually identify the work of an individual thatcher: his roof would carry his 'signature'; it would differ in some detail from any other roof by any other thatcher. It might be some detail of ornamenta-tion high up near the ridge of the roof or round the chimneys; it might be some peculiarity in the way the thatch was fitted and bedded round the dormer windows; it might be the trimming at the eaves. Or it might be a matter of choice of material for decorative purposes. A certain thatcher, for example, might have a fancy for using lengths of bramble to weave a pattern among his dog-tooth hazel spars. It is never wise to assume that a country-man is lacking in imagination just because he works to an old tradition and appears to move slowly in everything that he does.

Another sign of the individuality of the thatcher lies in the fact that he usually makes his own tools; or if he cannot manage this, then has them made to his own special and highly individual taste by the local blacksmith. An expert could probably distinguish between the tools of one thatcher and those of another in a village a mile or two away; the ordinary person would probably see nothing individual about them. But put someone else's tools into the hands of a blindfolded thatcher and he will know they are not his almost before his fingers have closed round their handles! Something about their weight, 'handiness', balance, length of handle, or the texture of the wood or metal of which they are made, would reveal the truth to him in a flash. No craftsman, whether joiner, clog maker, chair bodger, trug maker or

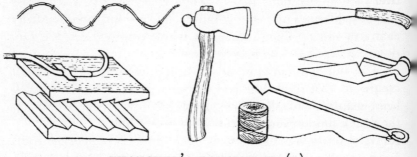

THATCHER'S EQUIPMENT (I)

snaith maker, is more particular about his tools than a thatcher is, even though his tools seem primitive by almost any standards.

These tools are few, but essential. The most important of them is the 'beetle', which differs very considerably from the many beetles used by other workers in timber. It is a square, heavy piece of wood with a strongly grooved surface and mounted on a short, stout handle. A wrought-iron hook is set in the back of it so that the thatcher can lay it down on a steeply sloping 'strake' of thatch without fear of its sliding to the ground and so having to be retrieved before he can continue his work. It is rare to find two identical beetles. Some have a 'ridge-and-furrow' surface on their working-face, others have small corrugations, others are indented diagonally, others again have a criss-cross pattern. The object is to have a surface that will enable the thatcher to beat the butt ends of his 'thraves'—or bundles of straw or reed—upwards so that the tapering ends are driven well home into those above them when the time comes to finish off the roof.

He carries a tool which is part hatchet, part hammer, and is known to him as his 'shingling-hammer'; this is useful when there is an on-the-spot repair job to be done on the battens or other woodwork in the roof before the thatch can be laid. He uses a pair of sheep-shears for trimming loose ends of straw, particularly at the eaves. These shears are capable of being given a razor-like edge, and the thatcher ordinarily keeps a noose of leather fitted over them so that they can be stuck in his belt or pocket without risk of damage. That is the only tool likely to have been bought at an ironmonger's shop; but it is as likely that it has been handed down to him by his father before him.

The village blacksmith will have made, to his specifications, a couple of thatching 'needles'—long, harpoon-like affairs with heart-shaped points that enable them to resist the springiness of the thatch and stay in position until, with a deft flick of his powerful wrist, the thatcher jerks them out. But his most individual tool is his 'comb'. This is a miniature rake consisting of a few pegs driven into a frame for use in smoothing out straw or removing any tangles he may find in his thraves. He will have made it for himself, of proportions exactly suited to his mode of working.

In addition to his actual tools he will have two other pieces of equipment, again hand-made and highly individual though based on the traditional form. One of these is his 'carrier'. It consists of an ash stem with two long and nearly parallel prongs that make it resemble a giant tuning-fork. A noose of cord or even osier is attached to one of these prongs. When the bundle of straw or reed has been dropped down between the prongs the noose is slipped across the top, and the springiness of the ash keeps the noose tight and the straw secure while it is being carried from the ground below to where the thatcher is working.

Within handy reach, the thatcher keeps his 'holder'. This is a half-hoop usually made of hazel or ash fixed to a stout crossbar

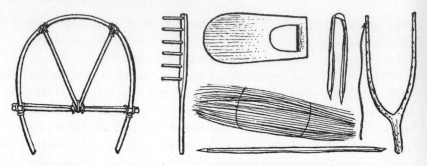

THATCHER'S EQUIPMENT (2)

and divided into three equal segments by 'spokes' of hazel or ash. In each of these three segments a 'thrave' of straw can be placed, leaving the 'carrier' free to continue his journeys up and down the ladder; thus the thatcher always has a reserve of straw ready to his hand.

His raw material, of course, is either straw or reed. In East Anglia, where the right kind of reed is plentiful and therefore transport and other costs are low, this is the more usual; elsewhere it is more likely to be straw, and will have come from oat, rye or wheat. The thatcher, however, invariably refers to the material in which he works as 'reed', and speaks of his bundles as 'reeds'. They may carry some special name, such as 'Wiltshire' or 'Somerset' reed, but basically they are all the same and are all applied to the roof in much the same way, with slight variations according to the individuality of the craftsman concerned.

The straw is very elaborately prepared for use. It is of course essential to have all the individual straws lying in line, not criss-cross, and with their butts all at the same end. The process of preparing the straw for use is given such names as 'reed-drawing', 'yelming' or 'gabbling'; but the principle is much the same throughout. The straw is taken up in large handfuls from the loose heap on which it may have been thrown, and methodically drawn through a roughly fashioned 'comb' in such a way that it is automatically bundled into thraves suitable for use. It may have had to be damped slightly first, if very badly tangled, in order that it shall not snap when the kinks are being straightened out.

The only other raw materials essential to his craft are the hazel spars—the 'spics', 'tangs', 'sparrods', 'roovers', 'brotches', 'splints', 'scollops' and 'withynecks' that we have seen being made by the worker in hazel. He will use enormous numbers of these giant 'hairpins' of hazel, together with a great deal of strong, coarse twine, often tarred in advance as a protection against the weather.

He works always from right to left, and, of course, from the eaves upwards to the ridge—just as the tile or slate layer does. Normally he lays two 'lanes', or 'strakes', at a time and he is very careful never to uncover more of the old thatch than he knows he can cover with new before he leaves off work for the night.

Like all countrymen, and almost all rural craftsmen, he works apparently very slowly; certainly he never shows the slightest sign of hurry. All his movements, whether up and down the long, slanting ladder, between 'holder' and 'strake', or when laying down one tool and picking up another in its place, are deliberate, calculated. He never makes an unnecessary movement; all he does is economically done. If you are watching him you may wonder whether he will ever come to the end of the great expanse of roof awaiting him; but if you go away and return in a few hours' time you will be astonished at how much he has done during your absence!

Taking up his first thrave, he lays it with the butt well down close to where the finished eaves will be and secures it to the batten or lath or other foundation—perhaps of brushwood, or old thatch—with a deftly placed noose of twine. He lays a second thrave close alongside the first, and perhaps brushes them over firmly with his comb to make them interlock and even-up the surface. A second, a third, a fourth pair of thraves will be laid, each a little higher than the pair before it so that the slope is roughly in keeping with the pitch of the roof itself; and each overlapping by the same amount and then driven well home with shrewd blows of the beetle.

It is essential that a thatched roof should be evenly compacted throughout its length and breadth, otherwise there is the risk that it will sag. This must be avoided, for as soon as there is a hint of sagging, rain will find this out and will begin imperceptibly channelling out a passage for itself from ridge to eaves. This will produce the 'weak link in the chain', and far sooner than ought to have been the case the roof will require attention. A well thatched roof of straw ought to last thirty or forty years, even fifty years; a roof thatched with first-class Norfolk reed may last almost twice as long—even more than the lifetime of the occupants of the house or the thatcher who laid it!

Like so many other craftsmen, the thatcher uses his eye, his sense of touch and his inherited skill, rather than gauges and measuring-rods. He uses no tool to test the consistency and the compactness of the thraves he has laid: they will be right—neither too compressed nor too loose. The tension he put on the twine, the pressure he put behind his beetle as he drove the butt-ends upwards and so consolidated the straw, is something that came instinctively to him; he would never be able to explain to you how he 'knows' that it is exactly right, neither too great nor too little.

Thatch has two outstanding advantages over all other forms of roofing: it is a perfect insulating material, keeping a house snug in cold weather and cool in hot weather; and it is so light in weight that only slender rafters are necessary, and lightweight walls, too, for there will be little of the outward 'thrust' that presents such problems to the builder who intends to use slabs of stone, as in Lancashire and Yorkshire, or even the heavy slates and tiles that are so common in most parts of the country. If it has a disadvantage, it is that it is ordinarily highly inflammable; but today it is possible to treat thatch so that it is hardly more likely to catch fire from a wayward spark than any other kind of roof will be.

The individuality of the thatcher is best seen when, having laid the bulk of his roof, he comes to the final stages. His last 'lane' has been filled, his last thrave set in position, pegged down and combed to merge into the ones next to it above and below and on either side. The spars have been set deep into the foundation, their natural springiness preventing them from being forced outwards by the thatch through which they have been driven. Only the ridge itself now remains: the last and all-important part of the whole roof.

The thatcher has calculated his thraves so that the last rows of them on each side of the ridge are laid with their thinner ends sticking upwards all along the ridge like a double fringe of stiff, golden hair a foot or two high. Sometimes, but not always, he will lay some straw lengthwise along the 'join'. The main thing he must do, however, is to fold the upstanding straw over, from side to side, interlocking the tapering ends exactly as your fingers are interlocked when you clasp your hands together. These over-lapping ends are then 'sewn' down on to the thatch on the sides opposite to those on which the butt-ends have been laid.

It is in the patterns that accompany this process of 'sewing' that the individuality of the thatcher is so well seen. There is, for example, the 'diamond' pattern which a thatcher produces by laying strips of cleft hazel or other thin wood, which he refers to as 'ledgers', criss-cross along the roof a little below the ridge on each side. These ledgers will be pinned down on to the thatch with small hazel spars at their points of intersection. Obviously there is hardly any limit to the variations on this sewing of thatch; the diamond pattern—known to the thatcher as 'diment-ing'—is probably the most popular one, but thatchers can vary the proportions at will. Or they can form a 'dog-tooth' pattern with their hazels and spars; or make a 'scalloped' edge, or an edge composed of alternating deep and shallow 'tongues'. Or an undulating line may be 'stitched' on to the thatch, the line con-sisting of long, tough, durable stems of blackberry or some other trailing plant, and additional variety can be obtained by inserting 'knots' of well spaced and nicely proportioned spars. It is every individual thatcher to his own taste.

In the last stages of thatching a roof the craftsman responsible for it is continually changing from tool to tool. The shaggy 'eyebrows' along the eaves and over the dormer windows have to be trimmed with his sheep-shears and perhaps levelled upwards with his beetle. Each 'valley' between gable and gable, or between dormer and sloping roof, must be checked over and over again to make sure that there is no bunching or thickening of the thraves. The comb is in constant use, levelling off here, smoothing there, seeing to it that there is no suspicion of a 'join' or gap between any two thraves. Time and time again the thatcher descends his long ladder and walks away backwards from the building on top of which he has been working, to make sure that all is as it should be; and time and time again he returns, climbs slowly up his ladder, and gives a finishing touch here or there, though the onlooker would have been prepared to state that there was nothing in the slightest degree wrong anywhere at all. It is easy to believe that very often during the years that follow the thatching he has done the thatcher will make occasion to walk past and cock an eye upwards to see how his thatch is 'wearing': he is not in doubt about its durability, for he knows the work and the skill that went into it; but he likes to keep an eye on an expanse of roof that is his own individual creation.

The thatching of ricks is less skilled work, but skilled all the same; especially when the ricks have to stand in open fields where they are exposed to strong winds. Many ricks today have nothing better than tarpaulin sheets over them—probably because there is no thatcher available in the district. Or the hay or straw may have been baled up mechanically and stacked high and rectangularly in cold 'Dutch barns' of tall girders, lattice-work and curved corrugated-iron sheeting.

All the same, you will still find in many districts where arable farming is carried on on a big scale ricks that are square, rectangular, oval or round, and thatched as perfectly as any house or barn.

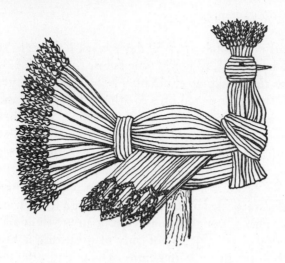

STRAW 'DOLLY'

And the chances are, in cases such as these, that some of the ricks will carry on their uppermost points or on their gable-ends straw 'dollies'. If you ever get a chance to look closely at one of these—and you will be lucky if you do, for they are likely to be far above your head unless you happen to come across the craftsmen who make them—do not miss the chance. For here is something in an old and dying tradition that beautifully illustrates the love of craftsmanship for its own sake that is found among the best types of craftsmen still working today.

The 'dolly' is the lowly cousin of the weathervane or weathercock, but it rivals its superior cousin in that, because it does not have to be made to turn in the wind, it can be of any strange and fantastic shape the craftsman's imagination and skilled hands care to evolve. It may be a 'cock', or indeed any sort of bird, real or fabulous. It may be a sceptre or some other regal symbol; or a horse's head, a conical hat, a cockscomb, a flag, a basket, a fish, a pair of horns—anything, almost, that you can imagine. But whatever form it takes, it is always made of straw; and of straw alone.

The craftsman who makes a dolly is not a specialist. He is very likely a labourer whose hands itch to be fiddling with something when he sits in his chair after his day's work is done, or straddles a stool in a barn while filling in time before the next job. It is easy to see how this tradition came into being. Just as some people 'doodle' with pen or pencil on a rough sheet of paper, and others whittle a piece of wood into some odd shape, and others again amuse themselves at the old game of 'cat's-cradle', so this man fiddles with loose pieces of straw. Manipulating loose straws turned into the conscious shaping of straw to produce something recognizable. Straw could be twisted; it could be plaited; knots could, with care, be tied in it. It was stiff enough to keep any shape given to it, pliant enough to use without any tools at all.

Many dollies are objects not only of great originality but of very real beauty. In most museums of country crafts there will be a display case, or shelf, on which specimens are preserved so that it is possible to see with what skill and fertility of imagination humble craftsmen such as these worked. No useful purpose was served by the making of these dollies—so that this particular type of craftsman was not *necessary* to the community in which he lived; but he enjoyed doing what he did, and the result of his handiwork was to give a sort of 'signature' to a rick which he himself had probably helped to build.

STRAW 'DOLLY'

Look at one close to and you will find that often it is as beautifully shaped as if it had been the work of a goldsmith, or a wood-carver working in some fine-grained timber like beech or box. The straw of which it is composed will have been plaited, twisted, braided, spiralled, bent and shaped without being broken, even though the craftsman's fingers are stiff and

126

thick and his movements clumsy compared with those, say, of a fitter in a factory where small, delicately machined parts are made and assembled. The dolly may be a few inches or a foot or more high; it may look like a fairy castle, a pepper-pot, a tree or a human or magic figure. And you might spend a whole autumn looking among ricks and never find two dollies that were the same.

Straw has always been cheap and plentiful, so that it is small wonder that the country crafts-man found many uses for it. Many countrymen keep bees, and though it may now be the fashion to house colonies of bees in factory-made hives of wood and glass and perforated metal gauze, there are still many bee keepers who prefer the old straw 'skep' which their forefathers used and which may still be found if you look far enough for them. These were made of straw 'rope', itself made of stranded golden straw which the skep maker produces by pulling gently at a bundle of loose straw while 'kneading' it lightly be-tween the fingers and thumb of his other hand. He can make a straw rope of indefinite length in this way; and it is the raw material of the skep, to the making of which he will turn when he has prepared sufficient rope for his purpose.

STRAW 'DOLLY'

The straw rope is wound, in the form of a continuous spiral, into the shape of a drum perhaps fifteen or eighteen inches across and about the same in height, tapering slightly outwards from top to bottom. At a little distance it looks as much as anything like a coil of new Manilla rope such as you may see on the floor of any ship's chandler. The proportions of the skep are obtained largely by increasing or decreasing the pressure or tension on the rope as it is spiralled round; but the rope must be, as it were, 'sewn' to itself all the way round as it spirals on its way. The

127

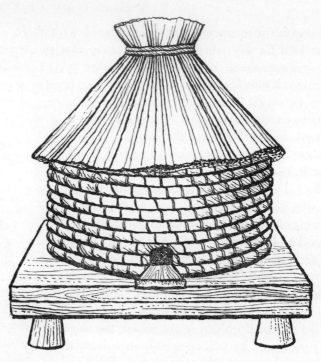

STRAW BEE 'SKEP'

sewing can of course be done with twine; but old craftsmen, and those who today maintain the old tradition, are more likely to use what they call 'splits'—fine strands of osier or hazel stripped off a stem and reduced by a sharp knife blade to a thickness about the same as that of packthread.

The making of this drum-shaped object calls for considerable skill. The continuous straw rope must be spiralled round, and the loose end of the 'split' threaded through the last spiral at regular intervals—often of no more than a few inches—and in such a way that when the spiralling is completed the diagonal 'stitching' on each run of the spiral fits in with the pattern of those that precede it. The craftsman has to do three things at once: keep an unbroken length of matching straws running through his hand, bond these together by twisting the 'split' round them as he goes, and increase or decrease the tension on the rope all the time in order to obtain the traditional curves and proportions of the skep he is making. As he approaches the top of the upward slope he has of course to increase the tension very considerably in order to fold it over and complete the domed roof.

He works sitting down, revolving the growing skep between his knees so that he can control its movement with a sideways pressure while building it up with the pull and movement of his hands. In fact, so tightly are the spirals of straw rope held together that he has to use a thin peg, or needle, of metal or hardwood such as box or beech, to force an opening for the end of each split, exactly as a cobbler uses his awl to make room for his waxed thread. When the skep is completed, and a wooden base made for it, with an opening for the bees to pass through, the whole thing is as rigid as if it had been made by a cooper of good oak staves. But it is light, well insulated from undue winter cold or summer heat, and—since straw is plentiful and cheap—it will have cost very little indeed to make and so very little for the bee keeper to buy. But he will have bought a craftsman-made article that will house his colonies of bees one after the other for many seasons to come.

Because straw was always plentiful, it was turned to good use by country workers of many kinds. It constituted the earliest type of mattress, after the housewife had begun to look for something better than just a layer or two of heather, bracken or brushwood. The shepherd, particularly at lambing time when he might have to remain out on chilly and windswept grazing-grounds for many nights at a stretch, used to make himself a complete mattress-bed of straw. Even today, in some of the remoter areas, the older shepherds still make and use these, though the practice is dying out gradually everywhere.

The 'straw bed' was made on exactly the same principle as the bee skep. The shepherd extracted from a bale of straw a continuous rope, which he worked into an elongated spiral. Kneeling on the ground, he worked the spiral round his toe and his knee, to give

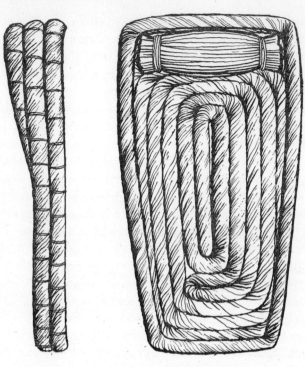

SHEPHERD'S STRAW BED

him length. As each spiral followed the previous one, he 'sewed' it with a 'split', or with a piece of packthread if he had any handy. The mattress was, of course, much longer than it was wide, as it had started with a long, thin section stretched between toe and knee. When it came to about six feet long, and perhaps two feet wide, he began to pull the rope a little tighter. This caused the last few spirals to rise a little from the floor. The result was that he had a mattress with raised sides to it: high enough at any rate to keep a little of the draught off him as he snatched a few winks of sleep between attending to one ewe and the next. Any straw he had left over he bunched into the rough shape of a pillow and tied with a noose or two of twine so that he had something on which to lay his head. This is an example of a craftsman in one sort of craft—that of shepherding—making use of the art of another type of craftsman—the skep maker—to bring a little comfort into his own work.

Straw, reeds and rushes are among the very humblest of the natural 'raw materials' in which country craftsmen have worked for centuries. Fewer and fewer example of their work are to be found each year; but those that are to be seen give a fine illustration of the way in which a material can be adapted to a purpose, and at the same time influence the craftsman while he is actually making use of it. The shape of the objects made with such materials is the direct result of their strength, weakness, texture and quality, and the craftsmen work with them remembering both their limitations and their serviceability.

Craftsmen in Elm

THE elm, which is one of our noblest-looking trees, often soaring to a height of a hundred and fifty feet and more and carrying a magnificent spread of massive and beautifully proportioned boughs and upper branches, possesses one quality that makes it unique among all our great timber-bearing trees. Though it has not the hardness and powers of endurance that oak possesses, and lacks the pliancy that is characteristic of willow and ash, it has a grain that offers a uniformly high resistance to splitting in every direction.

This is not mere toughness; it is due to the fact that in elm the grain runs, as they say, 'every-which-way'. A glance at the seat of a Windsor or similar type of chair will show this at once to be true. The grain pattern, brought out by years, perhaps even generations, not only of dusting and polishing but of rubbing by the seats of those who have occupied them, resembles as closely as anything the tangled contours on a large-scale map of, say, the Lake District. You might look at a thousand such chair seats and never find two that even remotely resembled one another in this grain pattern; they are as individual in their whorls and convolutions as fingerprints are.

This individual quality in elm, possessed by no other tree, has naturally led to its being used for certain purposes where no other timber would be selected by the craftsman unless elm were literally unobtainable. If he did have to use an alternative timber for his job he would be unhappy about it, knowing that it was no better than an 'also-ran'.

The wheelwright, though he uses oak and ash for various parts of the structure of his waggons, knows that his wheels, large or small, massive or lightweight, are built round hubs—which he refers to as 'naves' or 'stocks'. Stocks must have holes bored through them to take the axle ends, which inevitably means the removal of a considerable amount of the inner wood; and they have also to take a number of very close-set holes or slots for the inner ends of the spokes. There is only one timber that can be weakened in this way and yet stand up to the heavy wear-and-tear of use day in and day out over a period perhaps of many years. This is elm.

He picks his lump of elm 'from the round', if possible, buying as many baulks of the timber at a time as he is able to do, if he is sure that it is of first-class quality. He saws off a number of short, chunky sections from the elm logs, of varying girth, and stacks them for seasoning. This may take as long as five years, and during the period of seasoning the end-grain must be frequently brushed clean of the sap that has worked out to it, otherwise fungus will develop and the quality of the elm will deteriorate until it is of no use for the purpose of stock making. Sometimes the elm is bored out in advance, to hasten the process of seasoning; but the older wheelwrights rarely did this, believing that it was not fair to nature to interfere with the normal rate at which seasoning should take place.

When the elm was sufficiently seasoned for 'working' it was first very roughly hewn to shape with an axe or adze, the wheelwright's assistant turning it steadily while the keen blade trimmed it to the right proportions. After that it was placed on a lathe. Old-time wheelwrights used a massive but rather primitive looking wooden lathe consisting of wooden wheels of varying sizes geared to one another, the motive-power being supplied by the strong arms of a couple of apprentices swinging away at a giant handle like that of the old-fashioned mangle. Today there are better types of lathe available; but many wheelwrights of yesterday and of today preferred and still prefer to do almost the whole of the shaping of their stocks with adze, draw-knife and spoke-shave. With these simple tools the tough elm can, in skilled hands, be so perfectly shaped, rounded, fluted and bevelled that it is hard to believe the wheelwright did not use a lathe for the final stages of his work.

The hole for the axle is drilled out with an auger; the rectangular slots for the spokes are chiselled out while the stock is held rigid in a massive wooden vice, or, occasionally, on a horizontal spindle to which it can be locked in position while each slot in turn is sunk into it. The marking out of the positions of eight or a dozen or maybe sixteen such slots round the periphery of the stock calls for very great accuracy and skill. The space between each slot and its neighbour on each side must not vary by a hair's-breadth if the finished wheel is to run perfectly true.

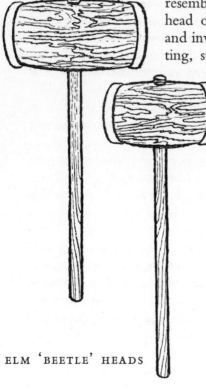

An object made of elm that closely resembles the wheelwright's stock is the head of a 'beetle'. Because this tangled and involved grain is so resistant to splitting, such a head will stand up to the shock of impact on post or wedge more successfully than a head made of any other timber, even oak. Big chunks of elm—perhaps of a quality just not good enough for wheel stocks— are roughly shaped with axe or adze, pierced with a big auger to take a straight ash 'stail', and sometimes fitted by the local blacksmith with a pair of iron bands shrunk on to each end while still hot. Beetles of ash and elm will drive in thousands of posts

ELM 'BEETLE' HEADS

or wedges with never a sign of a split, outlasting the lifetime of the man for whom they were made, and perhaps that of his son also.

Another characteristic of elm is its power to stand up to continuous immersion in water. Because of this, elm was much used in olden days for the pipes that carried water underground from source to consumer. Every now and then excavators in London and some other large towns come across the remains of a length or two of these elm pipes, long disused of course but still, after two or three centuries, fairly sound.

The craftsmen who made them used whole elm boughs while they were still 'green', that is to say unseasoned. They were first cut to convenient lengths, usually just less than twice the length of the augers with which they were to be bored. They were laid at a slight downwards angle on massive low trestles, and there locked in position so that they would neither shift nor turn when pressure was brought to bear on them. A yard or so from the end of the timber a 'rest' in the form of a forked branch was driven into the ground at a suitable height. This was to support the shank of the auger in the initial stages as the craftsman began boring his long hole through the elm.

The auger which a wheelwright uses is of course just an outsize 'bit' which can normally be fitted into his brace. He has a set of these, and the larger ones, too large to be used with a brace, are fitted with a longish shank with a hole or slot in the end, through which a bar can be thrust so as to give the user 'purchase' on his tool. They are, however, quite short, for the wheelwright is rarely likely to have to bore a hole more than, say, twelve inches long, even in the biggest of his stocks.

The craftsman who made the old elm water pipes, however, like his descendant today who may still be found making elmwood village pumps, used a giant auger. It would have teeth, or 'scoops', or 'shells' anything from four to six or eight inches in diameter. It would have a shank anything up to eight or ten feet long. To turn such an auger in tough, green elm timber called for great strength, and usually there would be an oak bar through the ring at the end of the auger shank on which two men could operate if necessary, though since boring with a ten-foot auger called for very great skill and judgment the craftsman would prefer to work alone on it, if possible.

He worked first from one end, judging his line down the heart of the elm by 'feel' rather than anything else, though the Y-shaped fork in which the auger shank turned would help in the initial stages to keep the 'shell' at the far end on its proper course. When his auger had penetrated so far that its handle was almost up against the butt end, he withdrew it, re-set the timber on the trestles, centred his auger again and began once more the slow and laborious process of turning it in the elm. By the time his handle had come close to it once more he would have reached the middle and the cutting-edge would have broken through to the hole he had bored from the opposite end.

The old elm pipes were laid end to end, 'nosed' into one another so that the water flowed freely along them. Today, of course, they have been replaced by metal or concrete pipes, but the tradition of the pipe maker survives in a few country districts where 'mains' water is still only a dream and every cottage has its well or pump. The elm on which the pump maker works is naturally much smaller in girth than the elm used for piping, but the tools used for its shaping remain the same. The long-shanked auger is used for boring out the cylindrical hollow that forms the body of the pump, and the 'bucket'—the plunger that rises and falls inside it like a piston when the long, curved handle is operated —is carved out of a chunk of elm and then fitted with a 'clapper'-type valve, often with a leather hinge.

The two main characteristics of elm—its reluctance to split and its resistance to constant immersion in water—led to its being the first choice of shipwrights for the keels of their ships. Enormous elm trunks were hewn with axe and adze and laid down between stem-post and stern-post; where a ship was designed that was too big for a single elm trunk, two or more such trunks would be laid down and locked together with what the blacksmith calls a 'scarf-joint'. Because of its resistance to splitting, any number of broad and deep slots could be cut along its length on each side to contain the lower ends of the oak ribs that formed the framework or skeleton of the ship, and the strength of the elm keel would not be in the slightest degree impaired.

Much of the piling in harbours and reclamation schemes, particularly where water and soft, wet mud are constantly present, is of elm; the groynes to be seen along those stretches of our sea shore where erosion is continuous are very often of elm; lock gates and similar heavy timberwork on our canals will often be made of elm. On a smaller scale, the wooden slats on water-wheels, technically known as 'floats' or 'strouds', are stout elm boards pegged to the rim of the wheel with oak pegs. The bobbins used on trawl nets where the lower edge has to trundle along the sea bottom are frequently made of elm: the timber will stand up both to the tremendous drag imposed by the resistance of the water to the forward motion of the boat and to the unevennesses of the sea bed itself. The 'dead-eyes' in a ship's rigging and the pulley-blocks are frequently made of elm, which alone will stand up to the strain of hauling on them and the ravages of wind and salt sea spray. Capstans, whether on ships or on quays—large bobbins through which four or eight oak or ash bars were thrust so that the men could get purchase on them when heaving up the anchor or warping a vessel in to her berth—used to be made of elm: it was the only timber that would not split when such tremendous twisting pressure was exerted on it.

Perhaps the most familiar use for elm, the one that is instantly recognizable, is the seat of the Windsor or similar type of wooden chair. A chair seat, though it is a homely object, is one that is continuously subjected to a variety of stresses. Mechanically speaking, a chair is not at all a sound proposition if any strain is imposed on it other than the sheer downward weight of the occupant. If he leans heavily backwards on it, he strains the back; if he tilts it, he strains both the back and the legs, for both back and legs are simply bars driven into holes or slots in the seat from the top or from the underneath surface.

A Windsor chair consists of a seat set upon four beech legs, joined by beech 'stretchers', and a slightly or fully curved back consisting of anything from six to sixteen 'rising-rods' and a central 'splat', or 'banister', also of beech, the whole bound into one unit by a length of ash that has been steamed and bent on a pegged frame so that it makes a sort of horseshoe shape with its two ends inset into the back corners of the seat. Beech for legs and stretchers and rods, ash for the 'bow', and elm for the seat itself: elm because it is the only timber that could be expected to withstand the stresses likely to be continuously imposed on it by the use of the chair throughout its life.

The seat is cut from a well-seasoned elm plank not less than eighteen inches wide and an inch and a half or so thick. It is first cross-cut so that the elm is about eighteen inches square. Then the chair maker takes up his bow-saw and very roughly shapes his square of elm to the traditional proportions: it will have its corners rounded off, its two sides very slightly hollowed (or, in the case of certain chairs, boldly rounded), its back made slightly narrower than its front edge, and a 'tongue' approximately four or five inches wide and an inch or two deep left protruding from the middle of the back to take the supporting struts.

This outline to the seat is completed with bow-saw and draw-knife, with perhaps a final smoothing by the spokeshave. The under surface of the seat is always left fairly rough—just as the saw left it when it was taken from the elm trunk at the sawmill. It is the upper surface of the seat that calls for the most highly skilled of the operations carried out by the craftsman who makes these chairs. And the tool he uses for this part of the work is, curiously enough, one of the heaviest and most clumsy looking of all: the adze.

If you look at the seat of a Windsor chair you will notice that inside a rim that runs across the back and part-way along the sides the surface has been very slightly hollowed out. There is a

'WINDSOR' CHAIR SEAT MAKER'S ADZE

gentle curve to it across the back that is subtly divided into two matching curves by an upward-sloping 'spine' towards the front. Into these matching double curves the lower sides of the thighs rest snugly. Though the degree of hollowing-out is only a matter of fractions of an inch, the difference in the feel of a dead-flat surface and the surface of a chair such as this can be instantly and positively noticed. These curves are a beautiful example of the craftsman's work, work performed with one of the oldest tools in the wood-worker's armoury, the adze that was used for shaping the oak timbers of 'kruck'-built houses and the great timbers of our 'Wooden Walls'.

The chair maker stands astride of the seat, which rests on the floor, held firmly in position by the inside sole of each foot. His hollow-bladed adze is fitted with a stocky handle. He swings this upwards to knee height or higher, and then brings it down between his legs with a calculated swing. Because the grain of the timber he is working in runs in all directions he does not need to work 'with' it, as the worker in most timbers must do. He can work inwards from each side in turn, stepping round the seat as he does so, the keen, hollow blade of his adze scooping out shallow drifts of elm with each swing as easily as you might scoop butter out of a half-pound block with the edge of a spoon.

Though his blows may seem heavy and haphazard he is in fact working with great cunning. He knows that he can always chip away a little more wood, but can never put back any wood that he has chipped away to excess. There is calculation behind every stroke of that keen, heavy blade. Yet when he has finished shaping the surface of the seat its curves will be so gentle, so smooth, that you would think he must have used some tool far more delicate than the blade of an adze.

Only when the seat is shaped and hollowed to its traditional proportions does the chair maker bore his holes. There will be a considerable number of these: two in the 'tongue' to take the lower ends of the struts; a slot several inches long across the back of the seat, just where the tongue projects, to take the lower end of the banister; a hole in each back corner, roughly rectangular but with one pair of sides curved into one, to take the two ends of the ash 'bow'; anything between six and sixteen smaller holes set round the back and curved corners of the seat to take the rising rods; and four bigger holes on the under side of the seat to take the upper ends of the legs.

To drill so many holes, of varying sizes, would be difficult enough if only their spacing had to be considered. But the holes have also to be drilled at a variety of angles. The holes for the legs, for instance, must be so drilled that the back legs are both pointing slightly backwards and splayed outwards; the front legs will also have slight splay, but not so much as the back ones. The many holes round the rim of the upper surface of the seat must be bored at different angles because the rising-rods have to be splayed

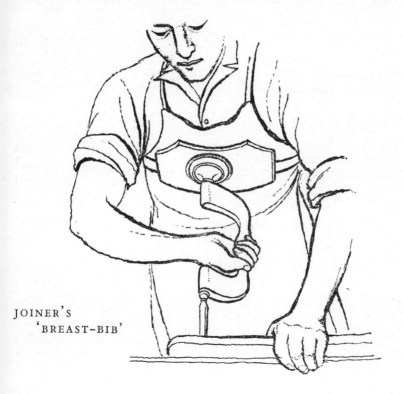

JOINER'S
'BREAST-BIB'

JOINER'S
'STOCK'

outwards to fit into the ash bow that knits them together and keeps them rigid.

To bore these holes the chair maker uses a brace, which he refers to as a 'stock', and a number of bits of varying diameters according to the purposes for which they are to be used. Because elm is tough the craftsman often wears what is known as a 'breast-bib'—a piece of wood with the inner side of it shaped to fit snugly across his chest and with a flattened hollow on its outer side to take the end of his 'stock'. He can thus exert considerable pressure without undue effort, and the stock is held more firmly in position that way than it would be if it was held with his hand alone while he turned it.

One thing you will have noticed already: whereas every timber of which mention so far has been made has been more often 'cleft' than sawn, elm is *never* cleft. Its wandering grain makes cleaving impossible. Take a wedge and drive it into a bole of elm with a heavy beetle and then try to cleave it: you will lose your wedge, because the elm will retain a vice-like grip on it however hard you smash at it. The craftsman working in elm knows better than to attempt to cleave it. If he did, he would be working against the very qualities in elm that make it invaluable for certain purposes; no craftsman ever wastes time or effort in his work.

Generally speaking, this quality of toughness, of intractability, makes elm of value to the craftsman working in a big way rather than to the humbler type of craftsman. Shipwrights, wheelwrights, railway-waggon makers, makers of the flat trucks, or 'trams', used for transporting heavy blocks of slate and stone in quarries, choose elm because they know it will stand up to brutal treatment indefinitely. Garden barrows are usually made of elm because they have to withstand rough treatment and being left out in all weathers, often with wet and rotting matter lying in them.

Stables and cowsheds often have their partitions made of elm because it is a timber that will stand up to the weight and the kicks of horses and cattle without splitting. The craftsman who has had to work with elm may have grumbled at the way in which it has blunted his tools and caused his chisels and gouges to 'bind' as he worked with them; but he has known all along that the finished article will be better than it would ever have been if it had been made of an 'easier' timber.

There is one use for elm still to be mentioned, and that is for coffin making. Many coffins, of course, are made of oak, and of other timbers; but elm has always been the choice of the country coffin maker, partly because of its resistance to decay once it has been buried underground. Partly also, perhaps, because of the beauty of the grain when it has been worked on by a craftsman prepared to take trouble with it in a good cause.

Old-time coffin makers, and many in country districts today, used to make what they called 'fish-tail' coffins, a word which describes their shape perfectly. These curved-sides coffins demanded a great deal of skill in their making, for elm does not bend too readily. The craftsman would begin by making a considerable number of narrow saw-cuts across the inner side of each side plank, a process which he oddly called 'saw-calfing'. Then, using either hot water or steam, he proceeded carefully to bend the plank until the edges of the saw-cuts closed on one another. On his judgment as to the number, position and width-apart of the saw-cuts depended the curve of the two sides of the coffin.

When they had been found to be right, the two planks were placed opposite one another over the bottom of the coffin and lightly attached to it. Then a small fire of elm chips would be lit on a sheet of metal or a slab of stone inside and this would 'draw' the planks into position. They would have beeen moistened first, and the effect of the heat on the inner side of the wet planks would

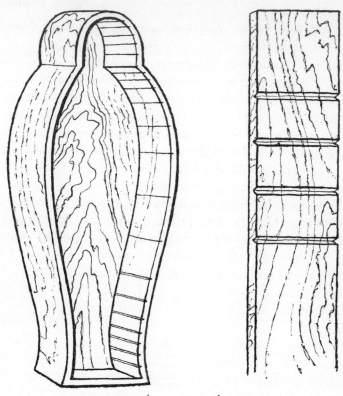

be to warp them to shape. By the time the moisture had dried out they would have 'set', and the coffin maker would then be able to put his screws or pins into their edges and secure them to the shaped plank forming the bottom. Then there would be the lid to be made, and the trimming and smoothing of the whole and the fitting of handles, with a final glass-papering to give the elm boards the right finish before they were varnished, and the job was complete.

The other type of coffin was one with what the craftsman called 'angled shoulders', which divided the two short upper sides from the two long, lower sides. This simply involved the careful jointing of straight elm planks, with reinforcement at the joints. Whichever type of coffin was asked for, it was usually—so far as the countryman was concerned—a matter of urgency. In the towns there would be ready-made coffins of various sizes, or they could be quickly made according to two simple sets of measurements, length and proportionate breadth. But the countryman preferred a coffin 'made to measure', so that the country coffin maker, who was often the local carpenter or wheelwright, would not have a stock in hand but would obtain his measurements and then work hard, perhaps throughout the night, to complete the coffin he had been called upon to make. As with everything else that he did, it would prove to be a true craftsman-made product, a simple container consisting of good planks of seasoned elm that had been stacked in a corner of his workshop against the day when they would be required.

Tail-piece

IT WOULD not be far from the truth to say that trees have proved as good friends to man as the horse and the dog: they have always been at his beck and call, and the uses to which he could put them have been explored since the earliest times right up to today. There are scores of timbers, and hundreds and thousands of uses for them, for which no room has been found in these pages. 'Treen', for instance.

This is the word used to cover all those thousands of small objects made by craftsmen for use in their homes—platters and bowls and spoons and tankards and drinking-vessels of every conceivable shape and pattern, no two alike. For these, all sorts of woods were used: the wood from fruit trees like apple, plum and pear and cherry; woods with beautiful grains, like walnut and sycamore; almost any wood, in fact, which grew handily, could be easily 'worked' with very simple tools, and would satisfy the craftsman's instinctive desire to make something at once useful and pleasing to the eye and sense of touch.

Anglo-Saxon craftsmen, for instance, used to make what were called 'methers'—mugs for drinking the national beverage of their day, known as mead. They were beautifully carved from a single piece of wood, often with three or four handles so that they could be passed from hand to hand down the long tables at ceremonial banquets. Welsh craftsmen used to fashion 'mazer' bowls, 'loving-cups' and 'wassail-bowls', often from maple wood, which has a very distinctive grain and texture.

The kitchens of country houses, and even of the humblest

cottages, would always be well equipped with a wide variety of wooden spoons, 'dippers', 'scoops', cream 'paddles', 'spurtles' and many other small, handy objects distinctive and original in shape and design, the work of some craftsman in his spare time. In certain parts of the country, for instance in Devonshire and Cornwall, where 'clotted cream' is traditionally made, the farmhouse and dairy spoons would be specially made with very flat, thin, tapered edges for the express purpose of sliding easily beneath the 'skin' of cream in the bowl.

The craftsmen who made these objects known as 'treen' were not necessarily full-time treen makers. In most cases they were craftsmen in some other country craft, perhaps not even connected with the use of timber, whose fingers had a natural itch to be 'making things'. A young man would often spend his evenings and other spare time in carving a set of spoons, from teaspoon to ladle size, as a 'matching set' to give to his sweetheart before marriage or on their wedding day. He might start only with the blade of his penknife and a piece of glass-paper or some other abrasive, and finish off what he had made by carrying it about with him during the day, smoothing it gradually by the sheer friction of a warm, rough hand. This would eventually give the object what the expert calls 'patina'—a surface difficult to describe but easy to recognize, and evidence of quality and age.

Eventually he would become more ambitious, buy a few simple tools, and begin trying out ideas in different woods, learning by trial-and-error which were the best woods for various purposes, and which were the best ways of manipulating the woods of his choice. His skill and aptitude would grow as he practised, and in time he would achieve a standard which gave his work a 'signature', so that it would be recognized by others as peculiarly his own.

Today, the numbers of craftsmen, at least those working in wood, steadily diminish. At one time, too, it seemed as though the population of our forests, woods and coppices, too, was likely to die out. Fortunately the Forestry Commission is seeing to it that there will always be sufficient trees in our land for all our purposes—and in spite of ours being a highly industrialized country nowadays, with more and more products coming from factory assembly-lines, some at any rate of these purposes are likely to persist indefinitely.

But the instinct to make things is something inborn in the great majority of us, so that there is no reason why craftsmanship in wood need ever wholly die. Wood is abundant; almost all of it, as we have seen, is comparatively easy to manipulate; wood-working tools cost little and, with careful use and maintenance, last indefinitely. The material, being a 'natural' material, exercises its own subtle but powerful influence over the craftsman who works in it, at once leading him on to experiment and checking his extravagances. And there are few experiences in life—as any craftsman knows, even though he may not often put it into words —more entirely satisfying than giving an idea form and substance in a material that is as much a living part of the world as the craftsman is himself.

 # Index

149

Index

Index